MARINADE EDITION 2

99 MARINATIONS, 99 TASTES

CHEF. YASH SHARMA

Copyright © Chef. Yash Sharma
All Rights Reserved.

Contents

Acknowledgements

Writing this book has been a significant journey, a whole year of busy schedule and special events with trials and errors of trying out all the following recipes which has made its way into this book. I would sincerely like to thank my family, friends, professors and colleagues for being so cooperative and enthusiastic in giving me their suggestions to complete the book.

Marination

Marinating is the key for preparing delicious meat and vegetable preparations.As marinating can be traced from various olden cultures of cooking where it is mostly used for grilling and baking food, but in today's modern cooking culture marination method is used also for smocking and sousvide cooking. To get the best out of marination, one must learn to use the proper amount and combinations of ingredients used for specific meat or vegetables. Also a right amount of rest is required to absorb and infuse the flavors while maintaining the required texture of the key products.

Marinade is also important as it gives base and flavouring to the dish before and while cooking. It is easy for an individual to use the marination method in day to day practice as it makes cooking less time consumable, tasty, easy to make and enhance your food experience. Marination intensifies the flavouring, act as preservative, makes meat juicy, induce lip smacking flavous in vegetables, prevents meat from drying out and becoming chewy. Marination time depends on the product and type of marination wet or dry, storage etc. For better results always use fresh ingredients, natural colour if required, the right amount of freshly ground spices and squeezed juices, air tight containers or vacuum seal bags etc. Use the remaining marinade for making sauces and gravies for the dish.

CHAPTER I

Seafood Marination's

KEY STEPS COMMONLY USED FOR ALL THE FISH MARINATION RECIPES ARE

- Always use fresh catch fishes.
- If you are buying fish from the local market, Check the fish before buying. See if the fish is fresh, see if the flesh of the fish is firm (when you touch the flesh it should bounce back) and it should have a shiny metallic colour, the scales on the fish should be firmly attached to the skin and not loosen.
- Clean the fish properly in cold running water.
- Use the back of the knife to scale the fish if required.
- Clean the inside of the fish and cut to remove all the inedible parts properly.
- Portion the fish sizes as required before marinating.
- I would suggest always fillet the fish and cut into portion size instead of using whole if not necessary.
- If you are ordering the fish online do check the quality & grading of the fish before buying.

• • •

Recipe 1 :

200 gm Basa fillet
20 gm Capers
10 ml Lemon juice
30 ml Olive oil
3 gm Lemon zest
2 gm Salt
2 gm Pepper

Preparation Method :

In a bowl add olive oil lemon juice, lemon zest, chopped capers and whisk it well. Add the fillets of basa fish to it and coat properly. Rest the fish marinating for 30 minutes before baking or pan frying it.

• • •

Recipe 2 :

200 gm Basa fillet
20 ml Soy sauce
30 ml Vegetable Oil
15 gm Thai chilli paste
5 gm Bird eye chilli

Preparation Method :

Slice the bird eye chilli and add it to the bowl with vegetable oil, Thai chilli paste, soy sauce. Dip the fish fillets in the marination and rest it for 1 hour before using it for cooking.

• • •

Recipe 3 :

200 gm Red snapper

10 gm Hoisin sauce

30 ml Fish oil

4 gm Honey

5 gm Five spice powder

2 gm Chinese pepper

2 gm Salt

Preparation Method :

Cut the fish into fillet. In a bowl add hoisin sauce honey, fish oil, five spice powder, salt and mix well to form a mixture. Then add Chinese pepper to it. Dip the fish in the prepared marination and rest it for 45 to 60 minutes before cooking it.

• • •

Recipe 4 :

200 gm Sole fish

40 ml Vinegar

5 gm Paprika

5 gm Cayenne pepper

2 ml Tabasco

2 gm Salt

Preparation Method :

In a bowl add vinegar, Tabasco, paprika, cayenne pepper and salt. Mix it and marinate the fish and rest it for 30 minutes before cooking.

• • •

Recipe 5 :

200 gm Baby octopus
15 ml Balsamic vinegar
30 ml Olive oil
5 gm White pepper
2 gm Salt

Preparation Method :

Clean the octopus properly before using it. Mix olive oil & balsamic vinegar in a bowl and whisk it well. Add the octopus to the marination and rest it for 1 hour before cooking it.

• • •

Recipe 6 :

200 gm King prawns
10 gm Garlic
30 gm Salted butter
3 gm Black pepper
5 gm Parsley
5 gm Paprika

Preparation Method :

Melt the butter and bring it to room temperature add chopped garlic back pepper, paprika and parsley to it. Clean and fully dry the prawns properly and add them to the prepared marinade. Rest it for 15- 20 minutes before pan frying them.

• • •

Recipe 7 :

250 gm Pink salmon
20 gm Mustard
30 ml Olive oil
10 gm Mayonnaise
5 gm Paprika
2 gm Salt

Preparation Method :

In a bowl add olive oil,mustard and mayonnaise mix it well. Then add red paprika and salt to it. Use the fillet of pink salmon and coat it well. Rest it in the mixture for at least 15-30 minutes before grilling or pan frying it.

• • •

Recipe 8 : Gravlax recipe

250 gm Smoked salmon
350 ml Beetroot juice

10 gm Honey
1 nos Cinnamon stick
3 nos Star anise
4 gm Salt
5 gm Black pepper

Preparation Method :

Use the freshly squeezed beetroot juice. Add honey,star anise, cinnamon sticks, salt and black pepper. Mix well. Add the smoked salmon to the liquid mixture and keep it for 2- 3 hours or over night in the fridge till the salmon becomes red in colour and all the flavors are absorbed. You can eat it directly or use it for making salads.

• • •

Recipe 9 :

200 gm Sole fish
15 gm Harissa paste
30 ml Olive oil
10 ml Lemon juice
10 gm Garlic powder
5 gm Pepper

Preparation Method :

In a bowl add olive oil, harissa paste, garlic powder, pepper and lime juice. Mix It well. Coat the sole fish fillets with the prepared paste and keep it marinated for 50-60 minutes before cooking.

• • •

Recipe 10 :

200 gm Bombay duck
15 gm Ginger garlic paste
20 ml Coconut oil
20 ml Vinegar
5 gm Cumin powder
5 gm Garam masala powder
3 gm Turmeric
5 gm Red chilli powder
2 gm Salt

Preparation Method :

Add coconut oil, ginger garlic paste, turmeric, cumin powder, Garam masala powder, red chili powder and vinegar and mix it well. Marinate Bombay duck in the prepared mixture and rest it for 40 minutes before using it.

• • •

Recipe 11 :

200 gm Prawns
600 gm Olive oil
10 gm Dried Oregano
5 ml Tabasco
5 gm Chilli flakes
2 gm Salt
2 gm Pepper

Preparation Method :

Mix olive oil and Tabasco in a bowl and add all the dry ingredients to it. Mix the clean & dried prawns to the prepared mixture and keep it marinated for 30 minutes before using it.

• • •

Recipe 12 :

200 gm Pomfret
10 gm Roasted Coconut powder
30 ml Coconut oil
10 gm Green chilies
5 gm Coriander
5 gm Mint
5 ml lemon juice
5 gm Garlic
5 gm Ginger
2 gm salt

Preparation Method :

In a grinder bowl, Add ginger ,garlic,green chilies,mint and coriander. Add coconut oil, roasted coconut powder, lemon juice to it as well and grind properly with the paste. Coat the fish properly with the prepared paste. Rest the fish marinated for a minimum of 30 minutes before cooking it.

• • •

Recipe 13 :

200 gm Red snapper
15 gm Red chilli paste
10 ml Lemon juice
20 ml Mustard oil
10 gm Garlic
5 gm Red chilli powder
5 gm Cumin
3 gm Black pepper
3 gm Curry leaves
2 gm Mustard seeds
2 gm Salt

Preparation Method :

In a bowl add mustard oil, mustard seeds paste, red chilli paste, curry leaves powder, red chilli powder, black pepper , cumin, lemon juice and salt. Mix well, coat the red snapper fish fillet with the prepared marination well. Rest for 1 hour before using it for cooking.

• • •

Recipe 14 :

200 gm Indian salmon [rawas]
30 ml Mustard oil
10 gm Jaggery
10 gm Ginger garlic paste
10 gm Green chilies
5 gm Tamarind paste
5 gm Red chilli powder

3 gm Peppercorns
2 gm Salt

Preparation Method :

In a bowl add soaked tamarind paste,ginger garlic paste, mustard oil, jaggery mix the mixture well till the jaggery dissolves fully. Then add chopped green chilies, red chilli powder and peppercorns to the mixture. Dip the fillet of the Indian salmon in the prepared marinade and rest it for 30 minutes before using it for cooking.

• • •

Recipe 15 :

200 gm Sole fish
15 ml Lemon juice
10 gm Mint leaves
30 ml Olive oil
5 gm Fennel leaves
5 gm Dill leaves
2 gm Salt
2 gm Pepper

Preparation Method :

In a bowl add chopped fennel leaves, dill leaves, mint leaves, lemon juice, olive oil, salt & pepper. Mix it well. In the tray place the fish fillets and pour the prepared marination on top till it coats the fillets properly. Cling wrap it and rest it for an hour before frying or baking it.

• • •

Recipe 16 :

200 gm Pink smoked Salmon

50 gm Butter

10 ml Lemon juice

5 gm Herbs powder

5 gm Mushroom powder

5 gm Onion powder

5 gm Garlic powder

Preparation Method :

Bring the butter to the room temperature or till the creamy stage. Add herbs powder, mushroom powder, onion powder, garlic powder and lemon juice and mix it well. Apply the prepared mixture on the fillet of salmon coating it properly. Rest it for 30 minutes before consuming it or using it for salads or cold cuts.

• • •

Recipe 17 :

200 gm Basa fish

30 ml White wine

10 gm Oregano stems

20 ml Olive oil

10 ml Balsamic vinegar

5 gm Thyme

2 gm Pepper

2 gm Salt

Preparation Method :

In a bowl add olive oil, balsamic vinegar and white wine and mix it properly to get infused. Add chopped thyme and oregano in it and season it with salt and pepper. Add the fillets of basa fish in the prepared seasoned liquid mixture. Cling wrap the marinated fish and rest it for 30-45 minutes before using it for cooking.

• • •

Recipe 18 :

200 gm Cod fish
25 gm Shallots
20 gm Yogurt
30 ml lemon juice
5 gm Dill leaves
5 gm Parsley leaves
5 gm Mint leaves
5 gm Garlic
2 gm Salt
2 gm Pepper

Preparation Method :

In a bowl add yogurt, lemon juice,finely chopped garlic, shallots,dill leaves, parsley leaves and mint leaves. Mix it and apply the prepared mixture on the fish fillets. Keep it marinated for 30 minutes before baking it. Served with pickles once cooked.

• • •

Recipe 19 :

200 gm Prawns
20 gm Red Thai chilli paste
30 ml Sesame oil
10 gm Lemon grass stalks
5 gm lime zest
5 gm Kafir lime leaves
2 gm Salt

Preparation Method :

Mix red Thai chilli paste, sesame oil and salt in a bowl. Add lime zest, lemongrass stalks and kafir lime leaves to the mixture. Put the d-shelled and d-veined prawns in the mixture. Marinate it for 1 hour. While using it for cooking remove lemon grass stock and kafir lime leaves. If you are preparing the gravy for the dish use it directly in stock for the same.

• • •

Recipe 20 :

200 gm Bombay duck
30 ml Olive oil
10 gm Green chilies
25 gm Red onion
10 gm Pecan nuts
2 gm Turmeric powder
5 gm Ginger powder

5 gm Garlic powder
5 gm Sugar
2 gm Salt

Preparation Method :

In a mixer grinder add green chilies pecan nuts, red onion, salt and olive oil. Grind it to a smooth fine paste. Add turmeric powder ginger powder and garlic powder with sugar in the mixture and grind it well. Apply the marinade to the fillet of Bombay fish and coat it well. Rest it aside for 30-45 minutes before using it.

• • •

Recipe 21 :

200 gm Hilsa fish
15 gm Dijon mustard
40 ml Olive oil
2 ml Tabasco
2 gm Salt
3 gm Pepper

Preparation Method :

In a bowl add Dijon mustard, Tabasco, olive oil, salt and pepper to make a marinade. Apply the prepared mixture on the Hilsa fish fillets for 30 minutes before using it for cooking.

• • •

Recipe 22 :

200 gm Bombay duck
10 ml Vinegar
30 ml Olive oil
30 ml Orange juice
5 gm Cinnamon sticks
3 gm cloves
2 gm Salt
3 gm Pepper

Preparation Method :

In a pan warm up the olive oil add cinnamon sticks and cloves to it. Once oil is cool down add vinegar, orange juice to it and season it well. Add the Bombay duck fillet to the prepared liquid mixture. Keep it marinated for 30 minutes before cooking it.

• • •

Recipe 23 :

200 gm Mackercl
20 gm Kashmiri red chilli paste
20 gm Dried coconut
10 gm Ginger paste
30 gm Tamarind paste
40 ml coconut oil
3 gm Turmeric powder
5 gm Coriander powder
2 gm salt
2 gm pepper

Preparation Method :

In a bowl add mix coconut oil, tamarind paste, Kashmiri red chilli paste together. Then add other ingredients like coriander powder ginger paste, dried coconut, turmeric powder and salt n pepper . Once the marinade paste is ready then coat the mackerel fish and keep it marinated for 30 minutes before using it for cooking.

• • •

<u>*Recipe 24 :*</u>

200 gm King fish
20 ml Lemon juice
40 ml sunflower oil
5 gm Chilli powder
5 gm Cumin powder
5 gm Coriander powder
5 gm Fennel powder
5 gm Cinnamon stick
5 gm Cloves
5 gm Bay-leaf
5 gm Nutmeg
3 gm Black pepper powder
5 gm Star anise
2 gm salt

Preparation Method :

Heat the sunflower oil, add bay-leaf, cloves,cinnamon sticks, and star anise. Get the spices fried in the oil and then cool down the oil.once oil is at room temperature add chilli powder, cumin powder, coriander powder, fennel powder, black pepper powder, salt and lemon juice. Mix well, add king fish to the prepared mixture for 30-40 minutes before frying it.

• • •

Recipe 25 :

200 gm Sole fish
40 gm Hung Yogurt
10 gm Green chilies
10 gm Garlic paste
10 ml Lemon juice
2 gm Salt
3 gm Pepper
3 gm Turmeric

Preparation Method :

In a bowl add hung curd, garlic paste, green chilies paste, turmeric, lemon juice and salt n pepper. Whisk it properly till a smooth mixture. Then add sole fish to the mixture for 40 minutes to get marinated.

• • •

Recipe 26 :

200 gm Basa fish
15 gm Jaggery
25 gm Tamarind paste

25 gm Onion
50 gm Coriander
5 gm Red chilli powder
5 gm Cumin powder
3 gm Turmeric
5 gm Garam masala
2 gm Salt

Preparation Method :

In a grinder bowl add halved onions, Fresh coriander, jaggery & tamarind paste. Grind it to a smooth paste. Then add all the dry ingredients to it red chilli powder, cumin powder, turmeric, salt and garam masala. Marinate the basa fish in the prepared mixture for minimum 30 minutes before using it for cooking.

• • •

Recipe 27 :

200 gm Fresh Salmon
10 gm Garlic cloves
15 ml Lemon juice
30 ml Olive oil
5 gm Garlic powder
5 gm Olive powder
5 gm Oregano
2 gm Salt
3 gm pepper

Preparation Method :

In a bowl add chopped fresh garlic, garlic powder, olive powder, oregano,lime juice, olive oil and salt n pepper. Coat the fresh salmon with the prepared mixture and keep it marinated for 45 minutes before baking it.

• • •

Recipe 28 :

200 gm Basa fish
20 gm Paprika powder
10 gm Green chilies
30 ml Olive oil
10 gm Garlic
5 gm Cumin powder
5 gm Coriander powder
5 gm Caraway powder
5 gm Mint
2 gm Salt

Preparation Method :

In a bowl add olive oil, chopped green chilies, garlic and mint. Add remaining powder ingredients like paprika, cumin, coriander,caraway and season it with salt n pepper. Coat the basa fish in the prepared marinade for 30 minutes before using it for cooking.

• • •

Recipe 29 : Pesto marinade

200 gm Smoked Salmon

100 ml Olive oil
30 gm Basil leaves
15 gm Spinach
4 gm Sea salt
5 gm Walnuts
2 ml Tabasco
2 gm Pepper
2 gm Salt

Preparation Method :

Heat the olive oil and add basil leaves to it for an infusion of flavors. Cool down the olive oil and add it to a grinder bowl with spinach, sea salt, walnuts, Tabasco and salt n pepper. In a tray pour the mixture add the smoked salmon in it and rest it overnight or for 12 hours like gravlax before serving it or using it in a salad.

• • •

Recipe 30 :

200 gm Red snapper
30 gm Corn juice
30 ml Olive oil
10 gm Garlic cloves
10 ml Lemon juice
15 gm Tomato paste
5 gm Paprika powder
5 gm Caraway seeds
5 gm Chilli flakes
4 gm Sea salt
3 gm White pepper

Preparation Method :

In a bowl add olive oil, corn juice, lemon juice, tomato paste and mix it well with the hand blender. Then add chopped garlic, caraway seeds, paprika powder, chilli flakes, sea salt and white pepper to it and mix it well. Put the portions of fillets in the mixture and coat well. Keep it marinated for 40 minutes before using it for cooking.

• • •

Recipe 31 :

200 gm Black cod fish
20 ml Extra virgin olive oil
15 gm Onion paste
10 gm Garlic paste
15 gm Tomato paste
20 ml Red wine
3 gm Cinnamon powder
5 gm Sweet paprika
5 gm parsley
2 gm Salt
3 gm Ground black pepper

Preparation Method :

In a bowl mix onion paste, garlic paste and tomato paste together with red wine and extra virgin olive oil.then add dry ingredients to it, sweet paprika powder, cinnamon powder, chopped parsley, salt and ground black pepper. Mix it well, add black cod fish to the prepared marinade for

30-40 minutes before cooking it.

• • •

Recipe 32 :

200 gm Australian Snapper
25 gm Onion
10 gm Garlic
10 gm Ginger
15 gm Red Thai chilies
75 ml White wine
20 ml White wine vinegar
5 gm Fresh Thyme
5 gm Basil leaves
5 gm Parsley
2 gm Salt
3 gm Pepper

Preparation Method :

In a mixing bowl add white wine and white wine vinegar with chopped onion, garlic, ginger, red Thai chilies, fresh thyme, basil leaves, parsley and season it with salt n white pepper. Add the portions of Australian Snapper to the mixture. Rest it in marination for 30 minutes before using it for cooking.

• • •

Recipe 33 :

200 gm Haddock

40 ml Sake

30 ml Mirin

10 gm Fresh Ginger

20 gm Caramelize onion paste

5 ml Soy sauce

Preparation Method :

In a bowl add caramelized onion paste, soy sauce, fresh grated ginger, mirin and sake. Mix this mixture very well. Portion the Haddock fish and dip it in the prepared mixture for around 40 minutes. Pan fry the fillet and use the remaining mixture for preparing the sauce.

• • •

CHAPTER II

Lamb /Mutton Marinations

KEY STEPS COMMONLY USED FOR ALL THE LAMB RECIPES ARE

- Always buy or procure meat from a trust-able vendor who has all the certification of quality check and halal meat.
- Check the meat before buying, it should be very tender and juicy, skin should be dry instead of sticky and does not have any odor.
- There should be no bruises, tears in the skin, discoloration, feathers and broken bone at all this could lead to make the meat dry while cooking.
- Fats on the meat should not be yellow as it shows that meat is not fresh. And it shouldn't fall apart easily while cutting it.
- Rinse in warm water, dry the meat properly before using it for the marination.

• • •

Recipe 34 :

250 gm Lamb meat
10 gm Dried red chilies
15 gm Green chilies
20 gm Almond paste
10 gm Garlic
30 gm onion
50 gm Yogurt
5 gm Cumin seeds
5 gm Garam masala
5 gm Ginger
2 gm Salt
4-5 strands Saffron
5 ml Milk

Preparation Method :

In a mixer grinder bowl add dried red chilies, green chilies, roasted cumin seeds, ginger garlic and onion. Grind it well together to make a paste. Add the prepared pastes with the yogurt, saffron milk, almond paste, garam masala and salt. Mix well. Add the lamb meat to the prepared marinade. And rest it for overnight or for 2 hours before using it for cooking.

• • •

Recipe 35 :

250 gm Lamb boneless
50 gm Greek yogurt

15 ml Vinegar
20 gm Ginger garlic paste
5 gm Curry powder
5 gm Bay leaves powder
5 gm Cardamom powder
5 gm Coriander powder
5 gm Onion powder
2 gm Salt

Preparation Method :

In a bowl add Greek yogurt, vinegar, ginger garlic paste and all the remaining dry ingredients. Mix well. Add the lamb curry cuts to the prepared mixture and keep it marinated for overnight or 12 hours before cooking it.

• • •

Recipe 36 :

250 gm Mutton boneless
150 ml Coconut milk
15 gm Dried chilli pepper
5 gm Cinnamon stick
5 gm Cloves
5 gm Coriander seeds
5 gm Black peppercorns
5 gm Cumin seeds
5 gm Fennel seeds
4 gm Green cardamom pods
2 gm Salt

Preparation Method :

In a pan add cinnamon sticks, cloves, coriander seeds, dried red chilies pepper, black pepper corns, cumin seeds, fennel seeds, green cardamom pods roast them together and grind it to a fine powder. Add this powder to the coconut milk with the salt and mix well. Add the mutton to the prepared marinade and rest it for 12 to 6 hours before using it for cooking.

• • •

<u>*Recipe 37 :*</u>

250 gm Lamb
60 gm Greek yogurt
20 ml Mustard oil
20 gm Garlic paste
10 gm Green chilies
30 gm Red Onion
15 ml Vinegar
3 gm Turmeric
4 gm Curry leaves powder
2 gm Salt
2 gm White pepper

Preparation Method :

In a mixer grinder bowl first add green chilies, ginger garlic paste, mustard oil and red onion grind I well.then add curry leaves powder, salt, white pepper, vinegar, turmeric and Greek yogurt and mix well. Remove the prepared mixture into a bowl and add Lamb to marinate for 2 hours before using it for cooking.

• • •

Recipe 38 :

250 gm Mutton
50 gm Korean hot pepper paste {gochujang}
10 gm Garlic
30 gm Green onions
20 ml Rice vinegar
35 ml Sesame oil
15 ml Soy sauce
5 gm Brown sugar
2 gm Salt

Preparation Method :

Finely chop the green onions and garlic, add it in a bowl with Korean hot pepper, brown sugar, rice vinegar, sesame oil, soy sauce and salt. Add the mutton to the prepared mixture and rest it for 4 to 5 hours to get marinated well before cooking it.

• • •

Recipe 39 :

250 gm Lamb leg
30 ml Sesame oil

15 ml Soy sauce

20 ml Mirni

15 gm Sesame paste

20 ml Chilli sauce

3 gm Schezwan pepper powder

3 gm Chinese 5 spice

Preparation Method :

In the bowl add the ingredients together and whisk it well. Put the lamb in the prepared mixture and marinade it for 120 minutes before using it for cooking.

• • •

Recipe 40 :

250 gm Lamb boneless

10 gm Onion powder

20 gm Garlic

30 ml White vinegar

60 ml white wine

8 gm Rosemary

5 gm Paprika

2 gm Salt

Preparation Method :

In a bowl add chopped garlic,onion powder, chopped rosemary, paprika, salt, white wine and white wine vinegar. Mix well and add the lamb in the prepared mixture for 2 hours before using it for cooking.

• • •

Recipe 41 :

250 gm Lamb
10 gm Garlic
20 ml Lime juice
50 ml canola oil
10 gm Sweet paprika
10 gm Cayenne pepper
20 ml Rice vinegar
2 gm Salt
2 gm Black pepper

Preparation Method :

In a bowl add rice vinegar, lime juice, canola oil, salt, pepper, sweet paprika and cayenne pepper. Marinate the lamb in the prepared mixture for an hour or overnight before cooking.

• • •

Recipe 42 :

200 gm Lamb ribs
60 ml Olive oil
30 ml Lemon juice
10 gm Sage
2 gm Salt
2 gm Pepper

Preparation Method :

Finely chop the sage leaves and add it to the bowl with olive oil, lemon juice, salt and pepper. Mix well and coat the ribs properly with the marinade and rest it for 2 hours before roasting it.

• • •

Recipe 43 :

250 gm Mutton boneless
30 ml Extra virgin olive oil
80 ml Dry Red wine
10 gm Garlic
4 gm Cumin
3 gm Chilli flakes
3 gm Oregano
2 gm Salt
2 gm Pepper

Preparation Method :

Mix wine and extra virgin olive oil together and add Roasted cumin, chili flakes, oregano and chopped garlic, salt n pepper. Rest the mutton for overnight in the prepared marinade before cooking.

• • •

Recipe 44 :

250 gm Lamb boneless

80 gm Yogurt
20 gm Mint
20 gm Basil
10 gm Garlic
2 gm Salt
2 gm White pepper
8 gm Green chilies

Preparation Method :

In a bowl add yogurt, chopped garlic, green chilies, mint, basil and season it with salt and white pepper. Mix well. Add lamb in the prepared marinade and rest it for an hour or two before cooking it.

• • •

Recipe 45 :

250 gm Mutton
50 ml Peanut oil
30 ml Lime juice
10 gm Coriander
15 gm Parsley
5 gm Honey
2 gm Sea salt
2 gm Pepper
4 gm Cumin
4 gm Paprika
3 gm Red chilli powder

Preparation Method :

In a bowl add peanut oil, honey and lemon juice mix it with a hand blender. Add chopped coriander and parsley with sea salt, pepper, cumin, paprika and chilli powder. Marinate the mutton in the mixture for 5 hours or over night before cooking.

• • •

Recipe 46 :

250 gm Lamb sirloin
60 ml Olive oil
30 gm Onion
10 gm Garlic
50 gm Tomato paste
10 gm Parsley
5 gm Smoked paprika powder
5 gm Coriander powder
5 gm Allspice powder
5 gm Cayenne pepper

Preparation Method :

Grind onion, garlic, parsley in a mixer grinder. Add it in a bowl with olive oil, tomato paste and all the remaining dry ingredients. Mix well. Add the lamb sirloin to the mixture and coat it well. Keep it marinated for 2 to 5 hours before baking it or pan frying it.

• • •

Recipe 47 :

250 gm Lamb

60 ml Olive oil

20 gm Mustard seeds paste

15 gm Garlic

30 ml Lemon juice

5 gm Thyme

5 gm Red pepper flakes

2 gm Black pepper

2 gm Salt

5 gm Lemon zest

Preparation Method :

In a bowl add olive oil, mustard seed paste, lemon juice,chopped garlic, thyme, lemon zest, and remaining dry ingredients. Marinate the lamb in the mixture for 6 hours before cooking.

• • •

Recipe 48 :

200 gm Lamb shanks

50 ml Virgin olive oil

80 ml Red wine

10 gm Garlic

10 gm Parsley

3 gm Kosher salt

2 gm Ground black pepper

Preparation Method :

Add olive oil, red wine, chopped garlic, parsley and seasoning of kosher salt and black ground pepper in a bowl. Marinate lab shanks in the mixture for overnight and roast it.

• • •

Recipe 49 :

250 gm Lamb shoulder
20 ml Apple cider vinegar
30 ml Orange juice
10 ml Chipotle hot sauce
10 gm Garlic
4 gm Cumin powder
3 gm Cinnamon powder
4 gm Coriander powder
2 gm Dried oregano
2 gm Salt
2 gm Pepper

Preparation Method :

In a bowl add apple cider vinegar, orange juice, chipotle hot sauce, chopped garlic and remaining dry ingredients together and whisk it well. Add lamb shoulder to the marinade for 6 hours or over night before cooking.

• • •

Recipe 50 :

250 gm Lamb boneless butterfly

20 gm Parsley
10 gm Rosemary
30 gm anchovies pickled paste
30 ml Lemon juice
50 ml Extra virgin olive oil

Preparation Method :

Mix anchovies pickled paste, lemon juice, extra virgin olive oil together. Add chopped parsley and rosemary to it. Marinate the lamb in the prepared mixture and rest it for 2 hours before using it for cooking.

• • •

Recipe 51 :

250 gm Lamb boneless
50 ml Olive oil
20 gm Fresh oregano
10 gm Garlic
60 ml Pomegranate juice
20 gm Shallots
20 gm Pomegranate molasses
5 gm Sumac
2 gm Salt
2 gm Pepper

Preparation Method :

In a bowl add olive oil, pomegranate juice, pomegranate molasses, sumac, salt, pepper and chopped garlic, shallots, oregano. Add lamb to the marinade for 6 hours before cooking.

• • •

Recipe 52 :

250 gm Lamb
50 gm Red onion
30 ml Lemon juice
10 gm Coriander seeds
10 gm Basil leaves
40 gm Greek yogurt
15 gm Kalamata olives
40 ml Extra virgin olive oil
15 gm Celery
10 gm Dates
5 gm Lemon zest

Preparation Method :

In a mixer grinder bowl add red onion, coriander seeds, basil leaves, Kalamata olives, celery, dates and olive oil grind them all together to a smooth paste. Add lemon juice, lemon zest to the mixture with Greek yogurt. Mix it well and add lamb to it to get marinated for 2 hours before cooking.

• • •

Recipe 53 :

250 gm Lamb
30 ml Grape seed oil

20 gm Miso paste
30 ml Sherry vinegar
15 gm Watercress paste
2 gm Salt
2 gm Pepper

Preparation Method :

In a bowl add miso paste, watercress paste, grape seed oil and sherry vinegar with seasoning. Mix well. The marinade will be sour and sweet then add lamb to it for 30 minutes to get marinated and cook it by grilling or baking method.

• • •

Recipe 54 :

250 gm Lamb
30 ml Malt syrup
20 ml Lime juice
20 ml Olive oil
20 ml Hung Yogurt
5 gm Dill leaves
5 gm Lime zest
2 gm Salt
2 gm Pepper

Preparation Method :

Chop dill leaves finely and add it to the yogurt. Mix olive oil, lemon juice, lime zest, malt syrup and seasoning in the yogurt mixture. Add lamb in it for 45 minutes before cooking it.

• • •

Recipe 55 :

300 gm Lamb leg
20 gm Garlic
40 ml Olive oil
20 ml White wine vinegar
5 gm Rosemary
5 gm Thyme
5 gm Parsley
2 gm Salt
2 gm Pepper

Preparation Method :

Chop garlic, rosemary, thyme, parsley all together then add it in the olive oil and white wine vinegar, salt n pepper. Mix it well. Marinade the lamb leg in the prepared mixture. And keep it marinated for 30 minutes before cooking it.

• • •

Recipe 56 :

250 gm Lamb boneless
30 ml Vegetable oil
20 gm Tandoori masala
30 gm Yogurt
15 ml Lemon juice
5 gm Cumin powder
5 gm Coriander powder

5 gm Garam masala powder
3 gm Salt n pepper

Preparation Method :

In a bowl add yogurt, oil, tandoori masala, cumin powder, garam masala powder and coriander powder. Mix well then add lemon juice and seasoning in it. Add boneless lamb to the mixture and keep it to marinate for an hour before using it for cooking.

• • •

Recipe 57 :

250 gm Lamb
20 gm Capers
50 ml Buttermilk
10 gm Garlic
10 gm Coriander
5 gm Fennel
5 gm Mint
2 gm Salt
2 gm Pepper

Preparation Method :

Chop the mint, coriander, garlic, capers and fennel together finely. In a bowl add buttermilk and the chopped mixture, salt n pepper mix well.add the lamb in the prepared mixture. Keep it marinated for 45 minutes before cooking.

• • •

Recipe 58 :

250 gm Lamb
30 gm Beet root puree
30 ml Olive oil
50 ml Dry red wine
5 gm Paprika
5 gm Thyme
5 gm Oregano leaves
2 gm Salt
2 gm Pepper

Preparation Method :

In a bowl add beetroot puree, olive oil, paprika, chopped thyme and oregano leaves, red wine, salt n pepper. Mix it well to infuse flavors. Add lamb to the prepared mixture and rest it for marinating for 60 minutes before cooking it.

• • •

Recipe 59 :

250 gm Lamb boneless
10 gm Paprika
60 ml Olive oil
10 gm Garlic
10 gm Parsley
30 gm Harissa sauce
3 gm Ground cinnamon
2 gm Salt

Preparation Method :

Mix paprika cinnamon powder, harissa sauce, olive oil, salt, chopped garlic and parsley in a bowl. Add lamb in the prepared mixture to keep it marinated for 45 minutes before cooking it.

• • •

Recipe 60 :

250 gm Lamb boneless
20 gm Apricot puree
30 ml Canola oil
10 gm Ginger
10 gm Coriander
10 gm Green chilies
2 strands Saffron
5 ml Milk
3 gm Nutmeg powder
3 gm Cardamom powder
5 gm Mint leaves
2 gm Salt

Preparation Method :

In a mixer grinder add green chilies,coriander, mint leaves, ginger, canola oil and grind it to a puree. Add apricot puree to the mint puree mix well. Add saffron to milk and put it in the mixture. Add remaining dry ingredients. Add boneless lamb to the mixture and keep it over night before using it for cooking.

• • •

Recipe 61 :

250 gm Lamb leg & shoulder
30 gm Onion
10 gm Garlic
30 gm Sweet pumpkin
10 ml Lemon
30 ml Olive oil
2 gm Turmeric
5 gm Chili powder
3 gm Coriander powder
1 gm Cardamom powder
2 gm Salt
2 gm Pepper

Preparation Method :

In a mixer grinder grind boiled sweet pumpkin, onion, garlic and make it to a puree. Add the puree in a bowl, add alive oil in it , lemon juice and all the remaining dry ingredients. Marinate the lamb leg and shoulder with the prepared mixture for 45 minutes before using it for cooking.

• • •

Recipe 62 :

250 gm Lamb shoulder
80 ml Canola oil
10 gm Ginger

10 gm Garlic
5 gm Garam masala powder
2 gm Cloves
5 gm Bird eye chilli
6 gm Brown sugar
3 gm Cumin
2 gm Pepper
2 gm Cardamom
2 gm Salt

Preparation Method :

Heat the canola oil, add cloves, cumin, cardamom, chopped ginger and garlic, slit bird eye chilli. Then bring the infused canola to the room temperate and add garam masala powder, brown sugar, salt n pepper. Mix well. Add lamb shoulder to the prepared marinade for over night before using it for cooking.

• • •

Recipe 63 :

250 gm Lamb
40 ml Olive oil
30 gm Onion
10 gm Garlic
20 gm Tomato paste
20 gm Hawaij spice mix
5 gm Lemon powder
2 gm Salt
2 gm Pepper

Preparation Method :

Finely chop onion and garlic to add in olive oil with tomato paste, hawaij spice powder, lemon powder, salt n pepper. Add lamb to the prepared mixture for an hour before cooking.

• • •

Recipe 64 :

250 gm Lamb
20 gm Shallots
10 gm Garlic
15 gm Worcestershire sauce
20 ml Olive oil
30 ml Red wine
5 gm Thyme
5 gm Dijon mustard
2 gm Salt
2 gm Pepper

Preparation Method :

In a bowl add olive oil, dijon mustard, red wine,Worcestershire sauce, chopped shallots, garlic, thyme and salt n pepper. Add the lamb to the mixture and keep it over night before cooking the lamb.

• • •

Recipe 65 :

250 gm Lamb boneless
60 ml Olive oil
10 gm Onion powder
40 gm Sour cream
15 ml Tarragon vinegar
5 gm Rosemary leaves
5 gm Dill leaves
3 gm Caraway seeds
2 gm Pepper
2 gm Salt

Preparation Method :

In a bowl add olive oil, tarragon vinegar, sour cream and mix well. Then add all the remaining dry ingredients with chopped rosemary and dill leaves. Add lamb to the prepared mixture and keep it marinated overnight before roasting it.

• • •

Recipe 66 :

250 gm Lamb
80 ml White wine
20 ml Black olives brine
15 gm Garlic
3 nos Star Anise
5 gm Honey
5 gm Rosemary
2 gm Pepper
2 gm Salt

Preparation Method :

In a bowl add Honey, black olive brine, white wine, star anise, chopped garlic and rosemary, salt n pepper. Add lamb to the prepared marinade for 45 minutes before cooking the lamb.

• • •

CHAPTER III

Vegetarian Marinations

KEY STEPS COMMONLY USED FOR ALL THE VEGETABLE MARINATION RECIPES ARE

- Always use fresh vegetables
- Clean the vegetables properly in cold running water.
- Peel the skin of the vegetable such as yam, red pumpkin, potatoes, Bottle gourd.
- If you are not peeling the skin, then thoroughly rub while cleaning to remove all the dirt on top of the skin.
- Cut the vegetables into bite size or as instructed in the recipe before marinating.
- Vegetables should be kept for a minimum of 30 minutes to marinate for better results.

• • •

Recipe 67 :

250 gm Cottage cheese
50 gm Red bell pepper
50 gm Ginger garlic paste
10 gm Tandoori powder
20 ml Lemon juice
3 gm Turmeric
5 gm Coriander powder
5 gm Cumin powder
5 gm Chaat masala
2 gm Salt
2 gm Pepper

Preparation Method :

In a bowl add ginger garlic paste, turmeric, tandoori powder, coriander powder, cumin powder, lemon juice, chat masala and salt n pepper. Cut the cottage cheese in to cubes bite size and coat it with the prepared marinade. Rest it for 30 minutes before roasting or pan frying them.

• • •

Recipe 68 :

250 gm Cottage cheese
50 gm Onion
50 gm Capsicum
60 gm Hung curd
10 gm Garlic
10 ml Vinegar
20 ml Cooking oil

10 gm Garam masala powder
8 gm Red chilli powder
3 gm Hing
2 gm Salt
2 gm Pepper

Preparation Method :

In a Bowl add hung curd, chopped garlic,red chilli powder, garam masala, hing, salt n pepper, vinegar and cooking oil. Mix it well. Cut the cubes of cottage cheese, onion, capsicum and add it to the prepared mixture. Rest it for 30 minutes before using it for cooking.

• • •

Recipe 69 :

200 gm Mushroom
100 gm Zucchini
15 gm Honey
50 ml Olive oil
5 gm Chilli flakes
5 ml Tabasco
2 gm Salt
2 gm Pepper

Preparation Method :

Clean the mushroom well with flour water before using it. Cut the zucchini in cubes the same size as mushrooms. In a bowl add olive oil, honey, Tabasco, chilli flakes, salt n pepper. Mix the mixture well. Add mushroom and zucchini in it and coat it well with the mixture. Rest it for 30 minutes before cooking it.

• • •

Recipe 70 :

250 gm Egg plant
40 gm BBQ sauce
20 ml Hot sauce
40 ml Olive oil
3 gm Oregano
3 gm Chilli flakes
2 gm Salt
2 gm Pepper

Preparation Method :

In a bowl add olive oil, hot sauce, bbq sauce, chilli flakes, oregano, chilli flakes, salt n pepper. Add the bite sized egg plant in the prepared marinade. Rest it for 45 minutes before grilling or baking it.

• • •

Recipe 71 :

250 gm Tofu
50 gm Red onion
10 ml Soy sauce
20 gm Chilli sauce
20 gm Cooking oil
5 gm Bird eye chilli

2 gm Salt
2 gm Pepper

Preparation Method :

Cut the red onion and Tofu in cubes. In a bowl add cooking oil, soy sauce, chilli sauce, sliced bird eye chilli, salt n pepper. Mix it well. Add tofu and red onion in the prepared marinate and rest it for 30 minutes before using it for cooking.

• • •

Recipe 72 :

250 gm Cottage cheese
100 gm Zucchini
60 ml Olive oil
30 ml Lemon juice
15 gm Garlic
5 gm Thyme
5 gm Rosemary
2 gm Salt
2 gm Pepper

Preparation Method :

In a bowl add olive oil, lemon juice, chopped garlic, thyme, rosemary, salt n pepper. Add bite sized cottage cheese and zucchini in the prepared marinade. Rest it for 30 minutes before using it for cooking.

• • •

Recipe 73 :

250 gm Mushroom
50 gm Shallots
100 ml Olive oil
30 ml Worcestershire sauce
5 gm Basil leaves
5 gm Oregano leaves
2 gm Salt
2 gm Pepper

Preparation Method :

Clean the mushroom and peel the shallots. Heat the olive oil and add basil leaves in it to infuse flavour. Bring the oil to the room temperature and add chopped oregano leaves and Worcestershire sauce, salt n pepper. Mix it well. Add mushrooms and shallots to the prepared mixture. Rest it for 30 minutes before using it for cooking.

• • •

Recipe 74 :

200 gm Bottle gourd
50 gm Asparagus
20 gm Honey
30 ml Olive oil
20 ml Balsamic vinegar
2 gm Salt
2 gm Pepper

Preparation Method :

Cut the bottle gourd and asparagus in bit size, add honey, olive oil, balsamic vinegar, salt n pepper in a bowl and mix it well. Add squash and asparagus in the prepared marinade and rest it for 60 minutes before using it for cooking.

• • •

Recipe 75 :

100 gm Carrots
150 gm Zucchini
30 ml Mirin
20 gm Hoisin sauce
40 ml Peanut oil
3 gm 5 spice powder
2 gm Salt
2 gm Pepper

Preparation Method :

Cut the carrot and zucchini in a bite sized cubes. In a bowl add mirin, hoisin sauce, 5 spice powder, peanut oil, salt n pepper. Mix well. Add carrots and zucchini in the prepared marinade and rest it for 30 minutes before using them for cooking.

• • •

Recipe 76 :

250 gm Egg plant (Brinjal)

30 ml mustard oil

25 gm Ginger Garlic paste

2 gm Turmeric

5 gm Red chilli powder

5 gm Cumin powder

5 gm Caraway seeds

4 gm Curry powder

2 gm Salt

2 gm Pepper

Preparation Method :

Slit the egg plant from all sides. Make a mixture of cooking, ginger garlic paste, turmeric, red chilli powder, cumin powder, caraway seeds, curry powder, salt n pepper. Marinate the egg plant with the prepared marinade and rest it for an hour before grilling it.

• • •

Recipe 77 :

250 gm Squash

60 ml Olive oil

20 gm Sage leaves

3 gm garlic Cloves

3 gm Fennel

2 gm Salt

2 gm Pepper

Preparation Method :

In a bowl add olive oil, chopped sage leaves and garlic, fennel seeds, salt n pepper. Mix well. Add squash in the prepared marinade. Rest it for 30 minutes before cooking the squash.

• • •

Recipe 78 :

250 gm Baby potato
50 ml Red wine
20 ml Red wine vinegar
5 gm Thyme
2 gm Salt
2 gm Pepper

Preparation Method:

In a bowl add red wine, red wine vinegar, thyme, salt n pepper, mix it well. Add peel baby potatoes in the prepared marinate and keep it for minimum 1 hour before using it for cooking.

• • •

Recipe 79 :

250 gm Cottage cheese
10 gm Tomato ketchup
15 ml Worcestershire sauce
30 ml Olive oil
3 gm Garlic powder
2 gm Black pepper

2 gm Salt

Preparation Method :

Cut the cottage cheese in the bite size. In a bowl add tomato ketchup, Worcestershire sauce, olive oil, garlic powder, pepper n salt. Coat the cottage cheese with the prepared marinade and keep it to rest for 30 to 40 minutes before grilling. Use the remaining marinate for the sauce.

• • •

Recipe 80 :

250 gm Zucchini
25 gm Sweet bean sauce
25 gm Chilli bean sauce
20 ml Sesame oil
2 gm Kafir lime leaves
2 gm Pepper
2 gm Salt

Preparation Method :

In a bowl add sesame oil, sweet bean and chilli bean sauce, kafir lime leaves, salt n pepper. Mix it well. Add bite sized zucchini in the marinade and rest it for 30 minutes before using it for cooking.

• • •

Recipe 81 :

250 gm Tofu
40 gm Teriyaki sauce
10 ml Dark soy sauce
25 ml Mirin
5 gm Red thai chilli
2 gm Salt

Preparation Method :

In a bowl add teriyaki sauce, dark soy sauce, mirin, red thai chilli paste and salt. Mix well. Add cube sized tofu in the prepared marinade and rest it for 30 minutes before stir frying it.

• • •

Recipe 82 :

250 gm Button Mushroom
15 ml Soy sauce
50 ml Sake
20 gm Mentsuyu paste
5 gm Brown Sugar
5 gm Lemon grass
2 gm Salt
2 gm Pepper

Preparation Method :

In a bowl add sake, mentsuyu paste, brown sugar, soy sauce, crushed lemon grass, salt n pepper. Add cleaned button mushroom in the prepared marinade. Rest it for 30 minutes before using it or cooking.

• • •

Recipe 83 :

250 gm Soya chunks
15 gm Dijon mustard
20 ml Lemon juice
10 gm Capers
50 ml Olive oil
5 gm Dill leaves
2 gm Salt
2 gm Pepper

Preparation Method :

In a bowl add olive oil, chopped capers, lemon juice, Dijon mustard, chopped dill leaves, salt n pepper. Add boiled soya chunks in the marinade and rest it for 30 minutes before roasting it.

• • •

Recipe 84 :

250 gm Cottage cheese
15 ml Oyster sauce
20 ml Chilli oil
30 gm Bulldog veg & fruit sauce
10 gm Garlic
2 gm Salt

Preparation Method :

In a bowl add oyster sauce, chilli oil, garlic, bull dog veg and fruit sauce, salt n pepper. Add bite size cottage cheese in the prepared marinade and rest it for 30 minutes before grilling or roasting it.

• • •

Recipe 85 :

200 gm Asparagus
30 ml Hoisin sauce
10 ml Soy sauce
15 gm Mustard paste
30 ml Sesame oil
5 gm Honey
2 gm Salt
2 gm Pepper

Preparation Method :

Peel and cut the the asparagus in a bowl add hoisin sauce, soy sauce, mustard paste, honey, sesame oil, salt n pepper. Mix well. Add the asparagus in the prepared mixture and rest it for 30 minutes. Once ready grill it or pan fry the asparagus and use the remaining mixture for glazing.

• • •

Recipe 86 :

250 gm Yam (suran)

100 gm Hung Curd

30 gm Mustard oil

20 gm ginger garlic paste

15 ml Corriander

2 gm cumin

1 gm Nutmeg

2 gm Turmeric powder

2 gm Red chilli powder

2 gm Fennel seeds

2 gm Salt

2 gm Pepper

Preparation Method :

Cut the yam into the bite size. Add olive oil, hung curd, mustard oil and lemon all the spices, salt n pepper in a bowl and mix well. Add yam in the mixture. Rest it for 40 minutes and pan fry, grill it or bake it.

• • •

Recipe 87 :

250 gm Cottage cheese

15 gm Mint

20 gm Coriander

10 gm Green chilli

50 gm Yogurt

10 gm Garlic

5 nos Dry red chilli

2 gm Salt

2 gm Pepper

Preparation Method :

In a mixer grinder add mint, coriander, green chilli, garlic,dry red chilli grind it very well add the prepared paste in yogurt and season it with salt n pepper. Add bite sized cottage cheese in the prepared mixture and rest it for 30 minutes before baking it.

• • •

<u>*Recipe 88 :*</u>

200 gm Firm Tofu
50 gm Zucchini
50 gm Shallots
50 gm Orange puree
30 ml Orange juice
30 ml Vinegar
5 gm Star anise
5 gm Cinnamon stick
5 gm Paprika
2 gm Salt
2 gm Pepper

Preparation Method :

Prepare a mixture of orange puree, vinegar, orange juice and add paprika, cinnamon stick, star anise, salt n pepper. Add bite sized firm tofu, zucchini and shallots in the mixture and rest it for 45 minutes before grilling them.

• • •

Recipe 89 :

250 gm Pumpkin
50 ml Olive oil
5 strands Saffron
4 gm Sage
4 gm Tarragon
3 gm Chili flakes
2 gm Salt
2 gm Pepper

Preparation Method :

Heat the oil, add sage, tarragon and saffron in it and bring it to room temperature. Add chilli flakes, salt n pepper and bite size pumpkin to it. Rest it for 30 minutes and grill it. Use the remaining mixture for glazing.

• • •

Recipe 90 :

250 gm Cauliflower
15 gm Cheese powder
15 gm Garlic powder
40 ml Olive oil
3 gm Oregano
1 gm Nut meg
5 gm Paprika powder
2 gm Pepper
2 gm Salt

Preparation Method :

Clean the cauliflower with hot water and salt. In a bowl add all the ingredients together and mix well. Add cauliflower in the prepared mixture and rest it for 30 minutes before deep frying it.

• • •

Recipe 91 :

100 gm Bell pepper
150 gm Egg plant
50 ml Red wine vinegar
60 ml Green Olives brine
5 gm Capers
2 gm Salt
2 gm Pepper

Preparation Method :

Cut the bell pepper and egg plant in bite size. In a bowl add red wine vinegar and green olives brine with chopped capers, salt n pepper. Add the veggies in the mixture for 30 minutes and than grill it.

• • •

Recipe 92 :

250 gm Butternut Squash (red pumpkin)
60 ml Olive oil
20 ml Rice vinegar

10 gm Parsley
5 gm Garlic powder
5 gm Onion powder
8 gm Mint
2 gm Salt
2 gm Pepper

Preparation Method :

Cut the butternut squash into the bite size. Add olive oil, rice vinegar garlic powder, onion powder, chopped mint and parsley, salt n pepper in a bowl and mix well. Add butternut squash in the mixture. Rest it for 40 minutes and pan fry or bake it.

• • •

Recipe 93 :

250 gm Cottage cheese
60 ml Olive oil
15 gm Maggie masala
3 gm Turmeric
5 gm Chilli powder
2 gm Salt
2 gm Pepper

Preparation Method :

In a bowl mix together turmeric, olive oil, maggi masala, chilli powder, salt n pepper. Add bite sized cottage cheese in the prepared mixture. Rest it for 30 minutes and then grill it or pan fry it.

• • •

Recipe 94 :

250 gm Okra
50 gm Onion
50 gm Yogurt
3 gm Turmeric powder
5 gm Red chilli powder
5 gm Cumin powder
5 gm Coriander powder
5gm Chat masala powder
2 gm Salt

Preparation Method :

Grind the onion and add turmeric,red chilli, cumin, coriander and chat masala powders in it. Add yogurt, salt n pepper to the mixture. mix it well.slit the okra and stuff it with the prepared mixture. Keep it to rest for 3o minutes and then pan fry it.

• • •

Recipe 95 :

250 gm Bitter melon
20 gm Garlic
10 gm Ginger
40 gm Onion
50 ml Olive oil
10 gm Green chilli

3 gm Turmeric powder
5 gm Garam masala
2 gm Salt

Preparation Method :

In the grinder add garlic, ginger, onion, green chilli, olive oil and grind it well. Add turmeric, garam masala , salt n pepper to the mixture. Slit the bitter melon and stuff the prepared mixture in it. Tie a knot around it with a thread and rest it for an hour before pan frying it.

• • •

Recipe 96 :

80 gm Zucchini
80 gm Bell pepper
90 gm Mushroom
50 ml Olive oil
20 ml Lemon juice
15 gm Garlic cloves
10 gm Coriander
10 gm Parsley
5 gm Sweet paprika
5 gm Chilli powder
2 gm Pepper
2 gm Salt

Preparation Method :

Cut zucchini, bell pepper as the same size of mushroom. In a bowl add olive oil, lemon juice, chipped garlic, parsley and coriander, sweet paprika, chilli powder, salt n pepper. Mix it well. Add veggies to the prepared mixture and rest it for 30 minutes and roast it.

• • •

Recipe 97 :

250 gm Pineapple
30 ml Light Soy sauce
40 gm Light miso paste
10 gm Cayenne pepper
6 gm Garlic powder
2 gm Salt
2 gm Pepper

Preparation Method :

Cut the pineapple into bite size. Add light soy sauce, miso paste, garlic powder, cayenne pepper, salt n pepper. Mix well. Add pineapple to the prepared mixture and rest it for an hour. The grill the pineapple and use the remaining mixture for the glaze.

• • •

Recipe 98 :

150 gm Brussels sprouts
100 gm Mushroom
30 gm Red onion
10 gm Fresh parsley
60 gm Extra virgin olive oil

10 gm Aleppo pepper
30 gm Sherry vinegar
5 gm Lime zest
5 gm Fresh fennel leaves
2 gm Salt

Preparation Method :

In a bowl add olive oil, sherry vinegar, lime zest, chopped parsley, fennel leaves, Aleppo pepper and salt. Mix it well. Add Brussels sprouts, mushroom and red onions in the prepared mixture and rest it for 30 minutes before pan frying.

• • •

Recipe 99 :

200 gm Zucchini
50 gm Cherry tomatoes
15 gm Spicy mustard
40 ml Celery seed oil
5 gm Thyme
5 gm Oregano
5 ml Tabasco
2 gm Salt
2 gm Pepper

Preparation Method :

In a bowl add celery seed oil, spicy mustard, Tabasco, thyme and oregano, salt n pepper. Mix the mixture well. Add bite size zucchini and cherry tomatoes in the prepared mixture. Rest it for 30 minutes and then bake it.

• • •

70

www.ingramcontent.com/pod-product-compliance
Lightning Source LLC
Chambersburg PA
CBHW020749160726
47993CB00006B/2682

Dedicated to my parents,

Who taught me to Dream.

-   Shajahan N K

-   Bushara Shajahan

Contents

Preface

The purpose of this book is to make some understanding on quantum mechanics. Any people who have twelfth education can easily understand this book and this book will let them to create a foundation of quantum mechanics. We discuss from the origin to emergence of quantum computing. The basics in quantum mechanics is chosen as the framework of this book. I have omitted all the jargons that are usually played in quantum mechanics to make this book simple. I had also tried to get rid of maximum equation so that non science peoples can also enjoy this book. With some regret I have also omitted some quantum mechanical topics like quantum gravity hoping we can include quantum gravity in next or another edition.

This book is divided into 11 chapters on the condition of each topics. Every topics on this book is simple and basics of quantum mechanics. Images and graphs is necessary to understand what quantum mechanics is. We had included images and graphs for the better understandings.

Introduction

Imagine you are on road and a truck is about to hit you. By laws of motion in classical physics formulated by Issac Newton we can predict whether you can escape from the truck or will it hit you. If the truck is about to hit within how much time the truck will hit you, we can predict all these with laws of motion equations. But only on condition, we have to know some values like mass of truck, speed of truck your mass, your speed, by knowing values like these while we are observing we can precisely predict the future. Like this we can predict quantities like motion, path, time, acceleration of any classical objects by newton's laws of motion. The headache of classical mechanics was that it won't work for really small objects like electrons, atoms, and even molecules. This is not newton's fault, who developed classical mechanics. It's because physics behaves like this, even newton hadn't formulated such equations for tiny particles. In that small world of physics, there they follow another law of physics. Physics in this small world was described by quantum mechanics. In this book we start from the origin of quantum mechanics to the world of quantum computing.

"There is a saying common sense in quantum world is non sense in classical world and common sense in classical world is non-sense in quantum world."

1. Birth of Quantum Mechanics

In the beginning of 19th century scientists considered physics as a complete subject they thought everything in it has been found, nothing new to discover. Classical mechanics was completed by Isaac Newton's laws of motion and equations of gravity, James Maxwell taught us how to combine equations of electricity and magnetism, scientists like Rudolf Clausius explained laws of thermodynamics. So everyone thought that almost every aspect of physics was completed. Almost at this time scientists start to think about why heated metals eject light. As we know whichever metal gets heated, it will eject light (when iron rod gets heated it will glow in a reddish color). At that time scientists like James Maxwell suggested light as an electromagnetic wave. But heat is a thermodynamic property. There was no equation combining electromagnetic and thermodynamic properties. So they decided to study more about these two properties.

Heat is a measure of how fast atoms vibrates, for every particular temperature atoms vibrate in a particular state depending on how much temperature does the material have. Every vibrating atom has its own kinetic energy. All atoms in a material doesn't vibrate with same kinetic energy, it varies. Some may vibrate slower whereas some may vibrate really fast, as a result of this, every atoms doesn't have same kinetic energy. Therefore temperature of a material is the result of average kinetic energy of all atoms in that material. As an atom has its own vibrations, particles like protons, neutrons and electrons too have vibrations. Sub atomic particles like protons and electrons are charged which will be vibrated along with atoms. When charged particles vibrates it emits electromagnetic radiations. As electromagnetic radiations get emitted from these vibrating atoms naturally its energy will decrease gradually. This is how an iron rod emits electromagnetic radiation. Whichever objects have a temperature will emit electromagnetic radiation, but its temperature decides in which range the emitted radiation will be. We can't see every range of electromagnetic radiation.

We humans also emits these kind of radiations, our body temperature is 37 degree Celsius so with this temperature our body emits radiations which were in infrared range, infrared radiations are not visible with our eye, but with the help of an infrared camera we can see this radiations. A heated iron bar emits red, yellowish, orange, white light radiations these all radiations were in visible range that we can see it with our eyes.

As we said earlier every atoms in a heated material doesn't vibrate with same frequency, some may vibrate really slow, some may really fast. As a result of this, radiations emitted by these atoms will also be in different wavelength and frequency. Which means different range of electromagnetic radiations will be emitted from these atoms.

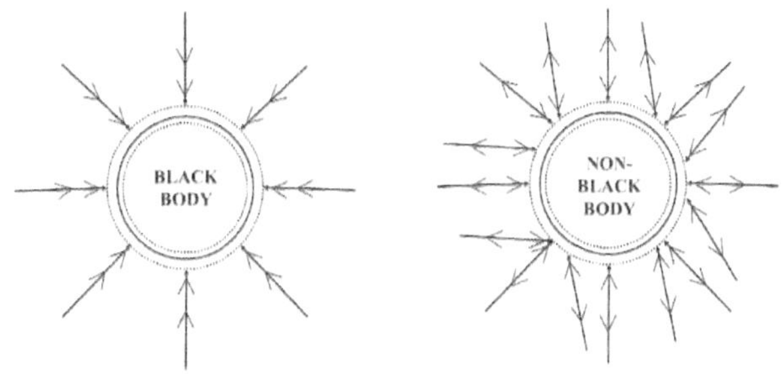

Black bodies are the objects which absorb all range of radiations. Similarly when heated, blackbodies emits all radiations of every single ranges. The radiation spectrum we get by heating a blackbody is what we call as a blackbody radiation spectrum. As the radiations emitted from blackbody is of from different wavelengths and frequencies, they will be emitted in different scales. Resulting a change in its intensity in the emitted radiations. If we plot a graph on the basis of how blackbody radiations are emitted it will look like this. The graph plotted here is called as a blackbody spectrum.

In the graph the X axis represent wavelength and Y axis represents intensity of radiations.

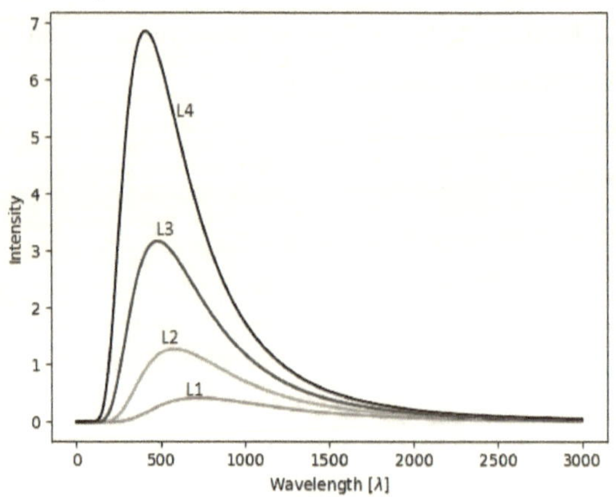

The curve represented by L1 (RED) shows graph of a metal which has a temperature of 3000 degree Celsius. These curves shows different range of emitted radiations anyways it includes very small range of visible range, its maximum intensity light lies in infrared region. The curve L2 (GREEN) has a temperature of 4000 degree Celsius and it overlaps visible range little more than 3000 degree Celsius, and its maximum intensity is in infrared but a little closer to visible region. The curve L3 (BLUE) shows about an object having 5000 degree Celsius, its maximum intensity lies in visible range. Which means when we heat this material at 5000 degree Celsius we can see the emitted radiations with our naked eyes. It also emits some radiations in ultraviolet region.

The specialty of graph like these is, as wavelength increases its intensity also increases and reaches its peak value as the frequency further increases its intensity decreases to zero. This will be the shape of all intensity vs wavelength graph.

In the beginning of 20th century Baron Rayleigh and James Jean decided to study more about the blackbody spectrum. They decided to study how wavelength and intensity depends on each other and they tried to formulate an equation relating these two properties. For this they used laws of thermodynamics and laws of electromagnetic radiation which was a part of classical physics. Depending upon the current classical physics at that time every objects can be divided into a large number of small infinite decimal quantity. That means let's assume, if I ask a number in between 1 and 2 probably you would say there is no number in between 1 and 2, but if we look carefully we can say after 1 there is 1.1, 1.2, 1.3… like this we can assume infinite numbers in between 1 and 2. Like as we did before, it is possible to divide any quantity to infinite amount, this was the concept of classical physics at the beginning of 20th century.

They postulated 2 points

*   As we said earlier, when we apply heat to a metal rod, its atoms will vibrate in different frequencies, some may very slow and some may vibrate very fast. Then they assumed, in between the slowest and the fastest vibrations there will be infinite number of vibration speeds in between them. For different speeds of vibration atoms will have different kinetic energies. If there were infinite number of vibration states, they assumed there will be infinite number of possible energy states, they tried to formulate equations on the basis of these.

*   They also assumed when an atom vibrates continuously it gradually loses its energy then it pass continuously through each and every possible energy state and stand on its lowest energy state

By using these two postulates they started to derive their formulas and equations. They integrated all energies in the continuous different energy states. Giving the equation

.

$$u_v = \frac{8\pi v^2 kT}{c^2}$$

u_v is the energy density, v is the frequency, k is Boltzmann constant, T is the absolute temperature, c is the speed of light.

When they plotted a graph as per the equation their graph is as shown.

When they plotted a graph as per the equation their graph is as shown.

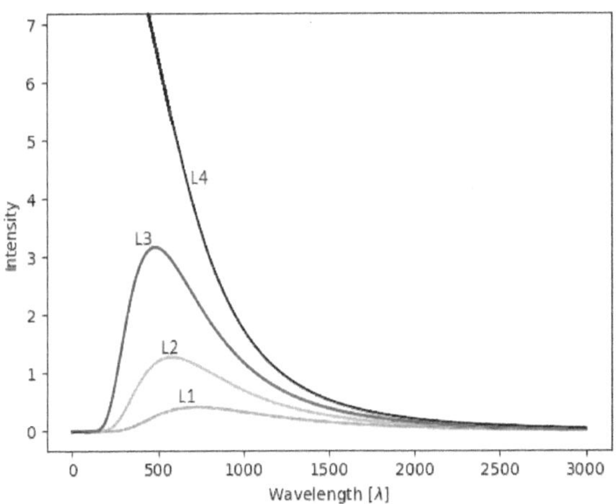

When we observe their graph we can see the lines L1 (RED), L2 (GREEN), L3 (BLUE) are the lines we got earlier [we got in practical experiment] and the line L4 (BLACK) is what Baron Rayleigh and James Jean get from their equations. Their graph was working when the wavelength was higher, but as the wavelength decreases, mainly wavelength below visible range graph tends to infinity. The graph they got from their theoretical predictions does not match, in the lower wavelength range it emits infinite amount of radiations. No material in nature will emits infinite amount of radiation. So they realized that there was some mistake in their equations, they checked the process again and again. They confirmed that there were no mistakes, they had used basic principles from thermodynamics and electromagnetism that their will be no chance for a mistake.

They felt that there was some problems in the equations which they were using, that's why even by using basic principles they were not able to get the accurate graph.

The mismatch between this theoretical graph and actual experimental results were later called as ultraviolet catastrophe. They found that the derivation they used in their equations was right, so they thought that the assumptions made by classical physics were wrong.

In 1901 Max Plank came up with a modification for Rayleigh and Jeans theory. Max plank said in between the slowest and fastest vibration states in atoms, there will not be infinite number vibration and energy states. Atoms can exist only with its minimum energy state and multiple of its minimum energy states. Which means atoms cannot have infinite number of vibration states as Rayleigh and Jeans said earlier, atoms will have a minimum energy states and its multiples. Max Plank explains minimum possible energy state of an atom is $E = h\nu$, next higher energy state is $E = 2h\nu$, next will be $E = 3h\nu$ and next is $E = 4h\nu$ and so on. Like this he assumed atoms energy sates can only be possible with the multiple of h. actually h was a new constant introduced by Max Plank. Earlier Rayleigh and Jeans integrated all the energy states of an atom but Max Plank corrected it, he said it's not integration, it's the summation operation that takes part. When Max Plank plotted a graph with his assumption he get a graph which is approximately equal to the experimental graph we get earlier. But the h was an assumed constant. At that time no one knows the value of h. even though when he plot the graph by standing h as an unknown value his graph matches with the experimental graph. As frequency increases the intensity of radiation also increases and reaches its peak, if frequency increases further its intensity will decreases and reaches zero. Max Plank got that bell shaped graph, then he find out the value of h by substituting several random numbers, he drew the graph every time until it become same shape of experimental graph. He again changed value of h and again drew graph until he get a correct shape of experimental graph. When he get the graph correctly he took that value as the value of h [value of h is 6.626 x 10^{-34}].

When Max Plank introduced the constant h, he

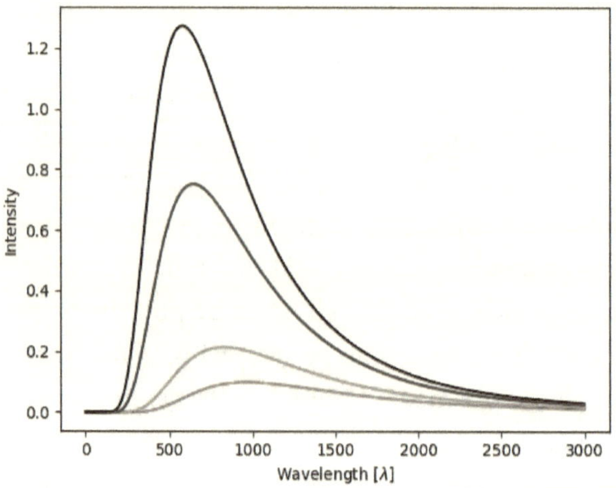

thought h is an assumed quantity so h will vanish when the formula was completed. But when the equation was completed h didn't vanished. It stand still in equation showing the assumed quantity was not only an assumption but a real quantity. Which means his assumed idea of energy state was not an assumption, it works in real world. This concept is known as quantization of energy. That means the energy state in atoms will only increase by each quantum, it increases step by step, it won't increase continuously.

When an atom comes to its lower energy state, it doesn't emits continuous electromagnetic radiation from higher energy state to lower energy state. It emits a quantum of radiation from a state then it jumps into its lower state, again it emits a quantum of radiation then again jump into its lower state, again when a quantum is emitted it jumps to its lower state. Which means for every jump of an electron it emits a quantum of radiation. In other words radiation is not a continuous emission, it is emitted as quanta. This was the assumption of Max Plank. This idea paved way for Quantum Mechanics. But Max Plank has no idea what was going on, that riddle was solved by genius Albert Einstein.

Einstein said the jump of electrons from higher energy state to lower energy state is because atoms can gain or release energy in the form of packets. Because energy was not a continuous flow, energy flows in quanta. That is why atoms cannot emit continuous energy when they jump from higher state to lower state. When an electron jump from its higher energy state to its lower energy state it actually emits a packet of energy known as photon. The jump of the electron will be equal to the energy of the emitted photon. Using this quantized nature of radiation, Albert Einstein was able to explain what photoelectric effect is. For the explanation of photoelectric effect Einstein got Nobel Prize in 1901. Max Plank also got Nobel Prize for the explanation of graph of blackbody spectrum in 1918.

By the discovery of blackbody radiation in 1901 by Max Plank and the explanation of photoelectric effect in 1905 by Einstein, by these two incident "Quantum Revolution" has started.

After that the assumed quantity h introduced by Max Plank was later known as Plank constant. Plank constant was an inevitable quantity in any quantum mechanics equation. We can see h in every quantum mechanics equations and operations. Value of h is 6.626 x 10^-34. Actually it is a very very small value. It is the value of h, which separate our real world and the quantum world. And also the reason for why quantum mechanics works only in quantum world is the value of h. which we will discuss through the book.

2. Double slit experiment

Modern physics especially quantum mechanics and its principles were based on the double slit experiment and the subsequent interference pattern.

In the 17th century, it was corpuscular theory proposed by Isaac Newton which was in effect at that time. Corpuscular theory defines light is a flow of small discrete massless particles know as corpuscles. Which helped Isaac Newton to explain refraction, reflection and transmission of light. [Refraction: Bending of light as it passes from one transparent medium into another, Reflection: Bounce back of light from objects, Transmission: Passing of light through medium without being reflected, absorbed or scattered.]. At the same time Christiaan Huygens also proposed wave theory of nature. But it was not popular as of Newton's corpuscular theory of light. In the beginning of 18th century an experiment was conducted by Thomas Young known as double slit experiment, as a result of his experiment he got an interference pattern. This experiment and its result changed everything that were hidden. Newton's corpuscular theory was unable to explain why this interference was formed instead of 2 bands of light. But wave theory proposed by Huygens was able to explain interference pattern which corpuscular theory was not able to explain, thus corpuscular theory lost its popularity and wave theory came in effect.

Let's understand what is double slit experiment. The image shown is the experimental setup of double slit experiment.

The source [part of system which emits light] we use in double slit experiment was a monochromatic light source [light only emits single color or wavelength] like laser in real life. The beam of this monochromatic light was then projected towards these two narrow slits. And the light which had pass through the narrow slits is allowed to fall on screen behind. We expect 2 bands of light similar to the slits on the screen. But their it appears a multiple band formed on the screen that follows

a pattern, the band formed at the center of the screen

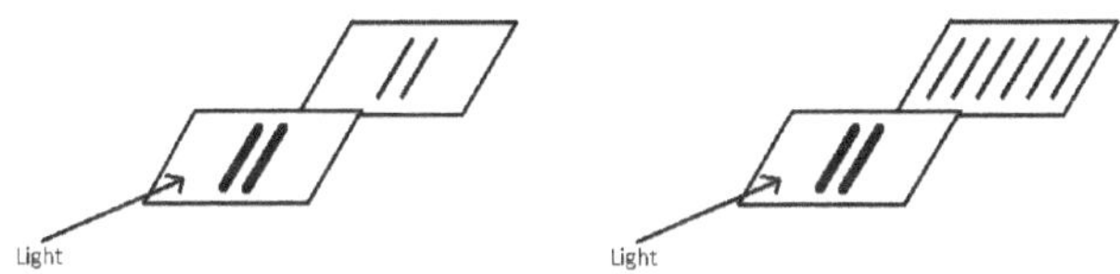

will have maximum intensity and as it goes on both sides its intensity decreases gradually as shown in figure (Figure from left shows expected and right shows result of the experiment). These bands are known as interference bands. Interference is a phenomenon in which two or more coherent waves superpose to form the resultant wave of lower, higher, or same amplitude. Newton's corpuscular theory was not able to explain.

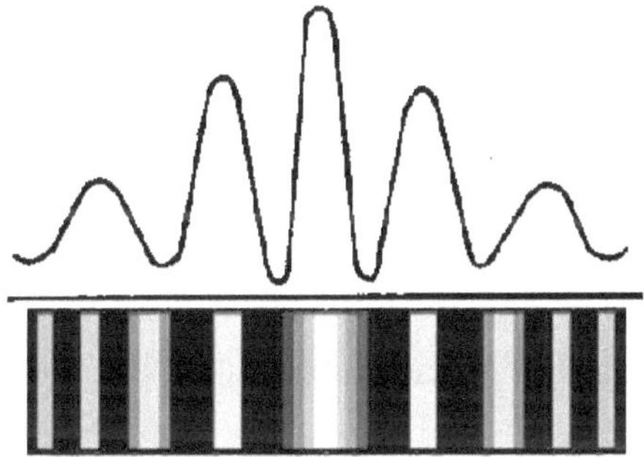

How these interference patterns are formed however Huygens wave theory was able to explain it.

To understand what is wave theory let's look at an example. Let's imagine a still pond. If we drop a stone in the pond. Waves will be generated from where stone was thrown. If we block these waves with a cardboard having 2 slits. Some waves will pass through the slits and other waves will be blocked by cardboard.

It looks like 2 new waves were originated from the slits itself. As these waves move forward these two waves which pass through the slit will merge together. Their crest and crest join together to form a higher crest, their trough and trough join together to form a lower trough. And when a crust and a trough joins it cancels each other thus no waves will be formed there.

The single coherent wave of light also behave like waves in water. When the light passes through the slits and travel as two newly originated waves. These newly originated waves interfere with each other forming interference pattern as we said before with the example of water. We get bright band where these two crests and two troughs meet that is shown in the figure in dark color. And waves gets canceled when one crest and one trough meets, at there we can't see these bands this region also called as dark band. This is how we get bright and dark bands on our screen. We get a continuous pattern which gradually decreases its intensity as shown in the figure. Here light behaves like transverse wave that is why we get multiple bands even light passes through two slits. These multiple bands are called as interference pattern.

After this, scientists repeated this double slit experiment with other particles such as electron, proton, atoms and even molecules. Each time when they repeated this experiment they get strange results. That is why double slit experiment became popular. Then scientists hypothetically concluded that all

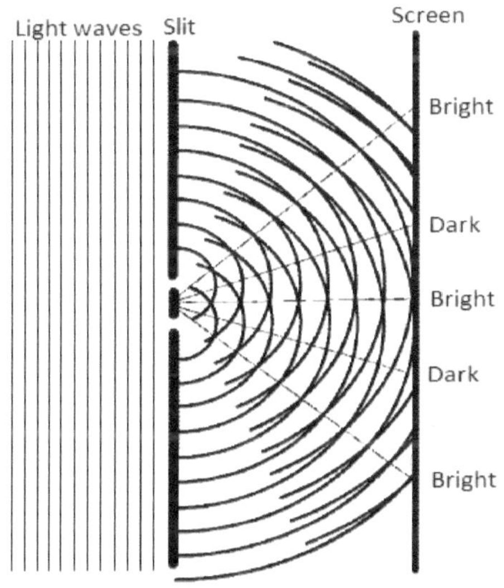

particles including classical particles can also behave like waves and result a diffraction pattern if and only if that object passes through a slit having an aperture nearly at the size of wavelength. But we know by de Brogle equation wavelength of massive objects is very very tiny. If a human being wants to be diffracted that human should pass through a slit nearly the size of 10^{-36} m. if humans pass through a slit of aperture 10^{-36} m they will form an interference pattern which was practically impossible. This concept that a particle can also exist as wave was a door for physics to enter into the new world called world of duality also called as duality principle.

3. Dual nature of matter

Earlier we saw, corpuscular theory of light was not able to explain interference pattern whereas wave theory was able to explain it. Which means particles were not able to create interference pattern, only waves can. Scientists repeated this double slit experiment again and again using different particles. They decided to do this experiment with electrons. We know electrons are matter, having mass and charge which revolve around nucleus. We didn't expect an interference pattern here because as we know electron is a matter.

Our aim is to generate electron using an electron beam, then pass it through two narrow slits, and observe the screen behind whether their forms a interference pattern. Scientists expected that no interference  pattern would be formed on the screen and they expected only two bands of electrons. But scientists found a shocking result, again they saw an interference pattern even if electron is considered as a matter. This results caused them some confusions. But they came up with a good explanation. Even though electrons are particles they travel as wave, they concluded electrons has particle nature as well as wave nature. The electrons from electron generators travel as waves. Some of the electrons will be blocked or reflected back and some will be passed through the silts. Those electrons which passes through the slits will continue its journey as a newly generated wave from the slits. And the newly generated waves interfere each other resulting an interference pattern on screen. Thus we get interference pattern on screen rather than electrons get concentrated on some region and form bands on the screen. This interference pattern is formed same as the waves in water forms.

Later the experiment was repeated not only in electron but also protons, neutrons, atoms and even small molecules. In all these experiments scientists got same result which is the interference pattern. With these results scientists got confused, they thought whatever result electrons shows, and they are actually particles. So they thought to form an interference pattern, at least one electron must be pass through each slit simultaneously. So they thought what happens if we allow to pass single electron through this double slit experiment at a time. Scientists get ready for the preparations of the next experiment. This experiment was called as "single particle double slit experiment". They setup the experimental setup as they done earlier, they made only one change. This time electron generator generates only single electron at a time. The electron generator emits next electron only after the emitted electron reaches the screen. So the emitted electron maybe blocked or maybe passed through any one slit then hits on the screen. Scientists eagerly wait for the results. After some time when they observe screen they get shocked again, once more they get interference pattern. Why did this happen? Scientists were not able to answer. Anyway how did interference pattern formed when only single electron was emitted at a time. Because to form interference pattern there should be 2 waves, here at one time only single electron was emitted. How did they interfere each other, how a single electron pass through both slits. Whatever happens if we emit single electron at a time it maybe bounce back or it maybe pass through any one slit only. Single electron can't pass through 2 slits simultaneously. And there is no electron passing through another slit to interfere with the emitted electron. Then how did single electron make interference pattern. There were some scientists concluded like, an electron travel as a particle and when it reaches the slit then it split into two and then passes through two slits as waves then these waves interfere each other to form an interference pattern. But majority of scientists were not able to accept this conclusion. Therefore it was necessary for scientists to find out through which slit the emitted electron passes. This took scientists to a new concept called as "which way experiment".

4. Which way experiment

The figure shown is the experimental setup of which

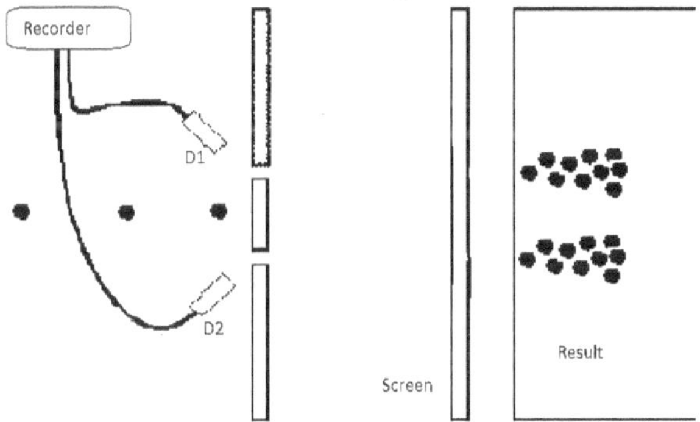

way experiment. The electron gun emits electrons one by one at a time. In between the screen and emitter, a board is placed with two slits in it. Detectors which can detect electrons were placed on each slits. The electron gun is placed as electrons can pass through any of the slits. The emitted electron maybe blocked or maybe pass through slit A or slit B. when electron pass through slit A the detector placed in slit A will detect the presence of electron and it will notify us. If the electron pass through slit B detector in slit B will notify us. By this setup scientist can understand whether a single electron can pass through two slits simultaneously. Now scientists clearly knew through which slit the electron has passed. They begin their experiment in this setup. Whenever electron gun emits an electron the detectors start to detect through which slit electron was passed. After the experiment was finished they observed the screen. This time they get two bands of electrons instead of interference pattern. This result really shocked them. They realized that somehow electrons understood that they were being observed by someone. So electrons started to behave in particle nature instead of wave nature. That is why this time we didn't get an interference pattern.

They repeated the experiment, this time the detectors was placed there but they were turned off. This time they got an interference pattern. This was really a weird result, when we observe electron they behaves in particle nature and when we don't observe they behaves in wave nature. Scientists noted that sub atomic particles behave in two ways when we observe and not. They were not ready to believe this theory. They questioned how electrons understood that they were being observed?

Some scientists blamed detectors. They said if detector can sense electrons somehow electrons too can sense the presence of detectors. This maybe the reason why we lose interference pattern. This was the explanation of some scientists. They started to think off new experiments to prove that they change their nature not because we are observing. Within that time not only subatomic particles, light also have particle nature and wave nature. Light is a flow of tiny packets or quantum of energy which was in particle nature, but they flow with wave nature this is called wave particle duality of light.

To understand further experiments, we have to understand quantum entanglement. Quantum entanglement was another concept in physics. When two particles are entangled they become mysteriously linked and when we measure some property like spin of one particle we automatically know the spin of its partner particle, even they are separated by several light years. Weird right? Imagine those entangled particles as coins they both will spin and finally one lands, if you see it's a heads now we know the other coin would be tails, guaranteed. We would talk about this later, now we understood that if we measure the properties of an entangled particle we can know the properties of its pair also.

Scientists were still trying to prove that electrons behave in particle nature not because we are observing. They decided to utilize the property of quantum entanglement in double slit experiments. There are some crystals known as BBO crystals, if one photon pass through this crystal that photon will be split into two photons having half energy each. These spited photons will be entangled pair. If we measure properties of one entangled photon we can understand properties of its pair. The newly arranged experimental setup is shown in figure

.

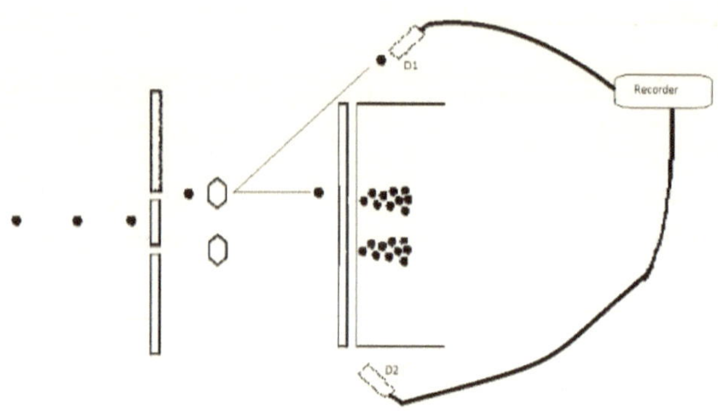

The light source emits only one photon at a time. The emitted photon may pass through any of the slits or maybe blocked or reflected back. Photons which pass through slit A will go through the crystal placed next to the slit A. This crystal spilt photon into two photons having half energy each. The splitted photons are entangled pairs. One photon in the entangled pair will hit on the screen and the other pair will hit on the detector. Thus with the help of this detector we can understand through which slit the photon has passed. If the photon from the source passes through slit B, it will go through the crystal placed next to the slit B. This crystal will also spilt photon into two photons having half energy each. One photon will reach the screen and one photon will be detected by the detector.

Scientists begin their experiment. This time they can find out through which slits the photos passed without interrupting or influencing the photon which hit in the screen. When they observe the screen there is no interference pattern this time also. Just like what happened in the earlier experiment photons somehow understood they are being watched. So they behave in particle nature. But this time they doesn't interrupt the photon which was going to hit on screen. Detectors only detected their entangled pair. Then how the photons in the screen understood they are being watched? This confused them a lot.

They again decided to repeat the experiment. This time they found a new way. This time the detectors were moved back, far from the screen. So the entangled pair which was going to hit on the detector have to travel a long distance than the photon which was going to hit on the screen.

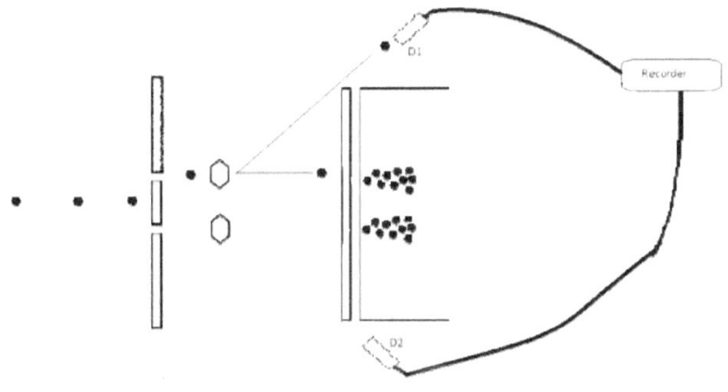

This time the detector can sense the photon only after the entangled pair hits on the screen. The photon which hits on the screen can't know whether the entangled photon was detected by detector or being observed, because photon which hit on screen will hit first. They started their experiment. But surprisingly this time also they didn't get an interference pattern. That means somehow the photon which hits on the screen get the information that its entangled pair was going to hit in the detector in future. Scientists get too confused. How the photons hit on the screen travel future in time and how they understood their entangled pair was going to hit detectors. Or the photons which hit the detectors travel past in time and informed their pairs, that they are being observed. It's an unbelievable result. Scientists said they can't believe this results. They again setup their experiments to prove that sub atomic particles change their nature not because we are observing. Every time they get weird results. At last they reached in "Delayed Choice Quantum Eraser Experiment".

5. Delayed choice experiment

Delayed choice quantum eraser experiment was conducted in 1999. The experimental setup was similar to double slit experiment. As before source was a photon gun which emits photos. That photon passes through slits. After that we placed BBO crystal to split the photon.

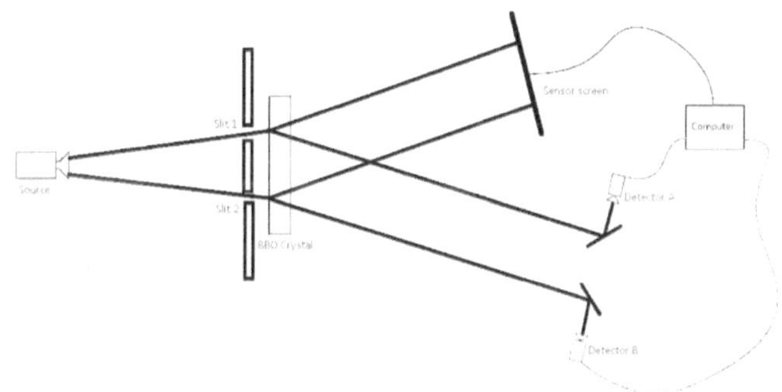

In this experiment they replaced the screen with a sensor. The sensor records when and where the photon hits the sensor or screen. This information was passed to the timing computer. And partially silvered mirror was placed in front of the detectors. Partially silvered mirror reflects and refracts 50 percent of photons. Which means half number of photons pass would through the mirror and half number of photonswould be reflected. Photons which had pass through the slits get splitted by the crystal and one of the entangled pair reaches the screen sensor and the other pair may pass through the partially silvered mirror and reaches eraser circuit or maybe it get reflected back to the detector, both the eraser circuit and detector was connected to timing computer. That means there is 50 percent probability for the entangled pair to reach eraser circuit or to reach detector. The same thing will happen for the entangled photon which passes through the other slit.

Let's see how it works. When a photon pass through a slit A, the crystal will split the photon and make it an entangled pair photon. One of the photon in the entangled pair reaches screen, it's time and position was recorded in the timing computer. The other entangled pair may reach in detector D1 or in eraser circuit, due to the partially silvered mirror, it's time, position and in which detector it was detected these information was recorded by the timing computer. Like that photon which pass through slit B the crystal will split the photon and make it an entangled pair photon. One of the entangled photon reaches screen and the other pair may reach in detector D2 or in eraser circuit, it's timing, position and in which detector it was detected these information were recorded in timing computer. If the photon was detected in detector D1, we can understand that photons were passed through slit A and no other photons will be detected in detector D1. Same as if the photon was detected in detector D2, we can understand that photon was passed through slit B. but if the entangled photon was detected in eraser circuit we have no idea through which slit the photon passed, because eraser circuit detects photons from both slits. When the experiment was completed, they observed their results. From the results they understood that at the time when photons was detected in detectors D1 and D2 it's entangled pair in screen was not in an interference pattern, at these times photons gives 2 band pattern like slits. But when the photons was detected by the detector eraser circuit, it's entangled pair gives an interference pattern in screen, in eraser circuit we have no idea through which slit photon had passed.

Which means whenever we try to understand through which slit photon passed or when we have the information through which slit electron passed, we get 2 band pattern. But whenever the information through which slit photon passed was hidden or unknown we get an interference pattern.

They get 2 postulates from this experiment

1. It is confirmed that sub atomic particles change its nature when we observe or when we have the information about it.

2. Photon which reaches in screen somehow gets the information what's going to happen in future.

Quantum mechanics work everywhere beyond space and time. They concluded.

6. Uncertainity principle

Uncertainty principle was proposed by Werner Heisenberg, he says that position and momentum or velocity of a quantum object cannot both be measured exactly at the same time. Actually it is not the uncertainty principle it is the possible explanation why it occurs. Instead let's look at what are the ways to understand what the principle actually says.

Now most commonly the uncertainty principle is described using the quantities of position and momentum. With these quantities were told the more we know about one, the less we know about the other. If we look at the equation the change in position is delta x and momentum is delta p then the product of these quantities together is greater than or equal to h by 4 pi. The h by 4 pi is a number, it's a constant. Which means the uncertainty principle is telling us that when we multiplied the two quantities together it should be greater than or equal to some number that means the product has to be at least this number. That means we cannot take the two quantities, momentum and position and make them both as small as we want. It says if one of the quantity is small the other has to get larger. So that when we multiply these together it has to be at least h by 4 pi. We can make one of them small at a time. We can't make one of them zero. If the uncertainty in the momentum is zero then the uncertainty in position has to be infinity. If we exactly know where the particle is with 100% certainly, then we absolutely know nothing about that particles momentum.

Imagine we are launching a rocket. A rocket has an exact trajectory and a path so that we can say its future, what will be the position of the rocket after a day, after a hour, after a minute, after a second, we can also say what will be the velocity of the rocket at these time. But that was not the case of an atom. We can't say the position and velocity of the electron simultaneously. When we talk about position and velocity(v) or position and momentum(p) both are same. Because for an electron its mass(m) is constant and equation of momentum is mass times velocity, as the mass is constant we can shift it to the right side of the equation.

$$\Delta x \Delta p \geq \frac{h}{4\pi}$$

$$P = mv$$

$$\Delta x \Delta mv \geq \frac{h}{4\pi}$$

Because on right hand side all the terms are constant

$$\Delta x \Delta v \geq \frac{h}{4\pi m}$$

Let's find out why we are not able to measure both position and momentum of an electron simultaneously.

Imagine if you are going to measure the thickness of this page of this book. Can you measure it with a ruler? No, because the least measurement that was available in our scale was 1 millimeter. The thickness of the page was less than 1 millimeter. We can't measure the thickness of the page with a ruler that we have. To measure the thickness of the page we must have a ruler which shows less reading than the thickness of the page. The minimum reading of the scale we are taking must be less than the thickness of the page. Then only we can measure the thickness of the page.

If we are trying to measure something, the instrument we used to measure must be having less dimension than the object. Here we are talking about electrons. The least count of the instrument should also be less than the dimensions of electron to measure the velocity and position of an electron. There problem arise, the electron itself is so tiny, building instruments which are having lesser dimensions than the dimensions of electrons was nearly impossible. That is why we can't measure position and momentum of electron correctly.

But still there is a possibility to measure the position and momentum of electron. If we incident a light with electron which have lower wave length than the wavelength of electron, we can measure the position of electron. We can identify the presence of electron If a light having wavelength less than electron hits on it, then we can understand the exact position of electron. But here's another problem. We measured the exact position of electron by hitting it with a low wavelength photon. If a photon hits an electron, the electron will absorb some amount of energy from the photon. Now the energy of the electron was increased, now it moves with an increased kinetic energy. We can't predict how much amount of energy does the electron absorbed. So that we can't say what's the exact velocity of the electron now. This happens instantaneously. That means we are able to measure the position of electron with light, but at the same time or simultaneously, we are not able to measure its momentum or velocity. This is what Heisenberg's uncertainty principle says. It is impossible to measure both position and momentum of a sub atomic particle at same time.

Now let's take the example of that rocket we had taken before, the exact position and velocity of rocket at any time can be measured, because it follows a path or it have a trajectory, that's why we can predict the position and velocity of rocket at any time. But in the case of electron as we are not able to find position and velocity of an electron revolving around nucleus. That means there is no an exact path for the electron around the nucleus. Which means nucleus was surrounded by a probability space where electron can be found. These spaces around nucleus was known as orbitals.

7. Quantum tunnelling

Quantum tunneling was one of the most useful phenomenon in quantum mechanics. Radioactivity decay, Photosynthesis, tunneling diodes, tunneling microscopes, fusion reaction in sun... these examples shows that how useful quantum tunneling for us.

There is an exaggerated analogy most common to understand quantum tunneling. Let's start with that analogy. It follows, if we through a tennis ball to a wall, it will knock and come back. No matter how many times we throw, it will knock back. But quantum tunneling says if we through a lot of times, means crores and crores of times there is a possibility that the ball will pass through the wall without breaking the wall. This is the most common analogy used to explain quantum tunneling. Even though this analogy explains quantum tunneling principle to a limit but it also exaggerate this principle to an extent. This analogy makes a misconception among us. Let's have a look an analogy to understand how this analogy mislead us.

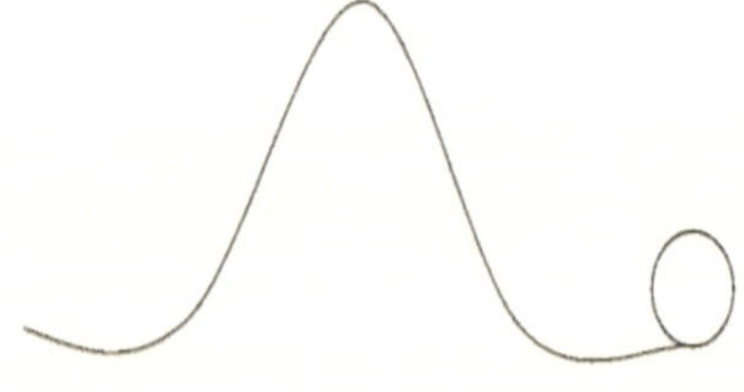

Let's imagine a small mound. If we roll a ball from one side to another side of the mound. The ball may go halfway and come back or the ball may pass through the top of the mound. In scientific terms, when we roll the ball we are applying a kinetic energy to the ball. Kinetic energy is the energy of a moving object. As the ball climbs the mound its speed decreases, as the speed decreases its kinetic energy also decreases. But energy should be conserved. Which means this decreasing kinetic energy was transferred into its potential energy. As the ball climbs the mound its height increases which leads to increase in its potential energy increases, but kinetic energy decreases. When the ball reaches the top of the mound it will have maximum potential energy, after that when the ball slides down through another side of the mound its stored potential energy was converted as kinetic energy and it rolls down. So it will pass the mound.

If we doesn't give the ball enough kinetic energy then the ball will go halfway and come back. If we again roll the ball without enough kinetic energy it will again come back. No matter how many times you try without having

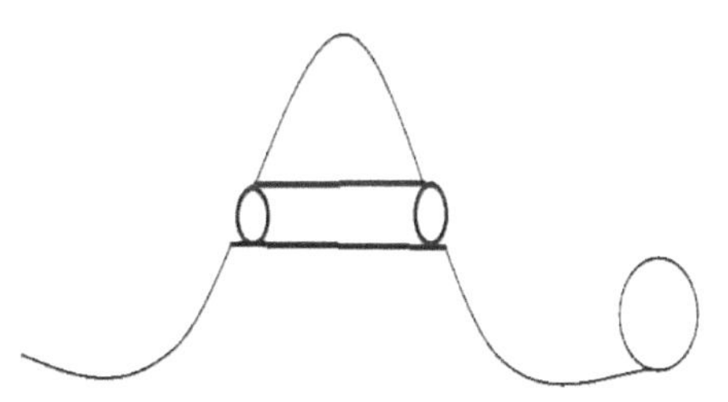

enough kinetic energy it will come back. It won't cross the mound without having enough energy. Now let's imagine there is a tunnel halfway in the mound, then the ball can cross the mound without having enough energy. We can relate this with the real life, so we can understand it. But what quantum tunneling says is, even if there is no tunnel, then we throw a lot of balls means crores and crores of balls, then probably some of the balls will pass through the mound.

Now let's understand, what is the difference between two analogies that we had discussed earlier. In the first case when we throw a tennis ball towards a wall, no matter how much energy we give to the ball, it won't pass through the wall without breaking it. But in the case of mound, if the ball is given enough energy, it will pass over the mound. That means it has a possibility. Quantum tunneling only works if there is a possibility. The examples we had discussed here is an analogy not an example. Because the things we used to discuss here [wall, tennis ball, mound, and ball] are not quantum objects. Quantum mechanics only work in quantum world. Which means no tennis ball are going to make quantum tunneling or no balls were going to quantum tunneling through the mound. Quantum tunneling only works on quantum objects. That is why we said these are just an analogy not an example.

Now let's look what is quantum tunneling in quantum world. To understand this let's setup an experimental setup.

Here we setup 2 negatively charged plates. We know 2 like charges repels each other. Like so here also those 2 negative charged plates will also repels each other. It's not just that their will be an electric field in between these two plates. We know to form a magnetic field it must need two poles, north and south poles. But electric fields can exist with one charge. So in between these two plates their will be a strong negative charged electric field.

Now let's setup an electron gun. As shown in figure. If we fire an electron from the electron gun, electrons are also negative charged particles. So electron will try to repel from the field. When it reaches near the field electron will repelled back. If we fire electron with more energy it will reach more near to the field. If we fire the electron with enough energy to reach at the center of the field then electron will travel near the center of the field. If electron was fired with enough energy to pass the center of the field, then the electron will pass the center of the field, that field itself will push the electron to the other side of the plate. Here what quantum tunneling say is, if we fire electron without giving enough energy to cross the center of plate, if we fire not one electron but crores and crores of electron like this. When we fire crores and crores of electron some of the electron will tunnel through the barrier field. That means when the electron reaches near the field, it will disappear from there and appear at the other side of the barrier and the journey of this electron will continue. This happen only if we fire crores and crores of electrons, then some of electrons will tunnel through the barrier, even if they don't have enough energy to cross the barrier field.

Now let's look at another scenario, if we rearrange the experiment with an infinite long electric plates. The electron can't cross the electric field as they are infinitely long, doesn't matter how much energy we had given to electron, because that barrier was infinitely long. In this scenario electrons can't tunnel, doesn't matter how much electron we had fired. Remember tunneling works only if there exist a possibility. Particles can't tunnel a barrier which was not able to cross.

This is why earlier we said tennis ball can't tunnel where ball rolling in mound can tunnel, remember only subatomic particles can tunnel.

Earlier we believed that tunneling was an instantaneous process. Have a look at the figure. If we fire electrons at same time.

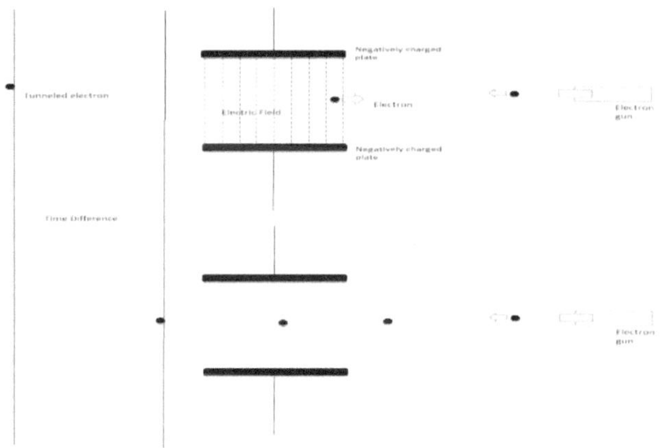

The tunneled electron will reach the detector earlier than the ordinary electron even they are at the same distance. This caused us to believe that tunneling was an instantaneous process, but on the later experiments we proved that tunneling also take some time. But it's very much faster when compared to the ordinary electrons.

8. Wave function

Let's go through an example to understand what a wave function is. Let's imagine a room which only have one door, room which have no windows and no other doors. Suppose there is a child sitting in this room, and his mother was standing outside the room. The room was arranged in a particular manner. Let's have a look in the figure.

A computer is placed one side of the room, beside that there is a bed, beside that there is a PlayStation, beside

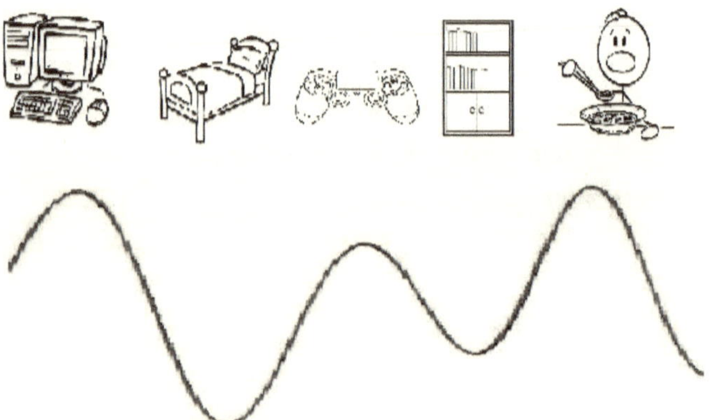

that there is a reading section, beside that there is some food.

If the child closes the door, then mother has no idea where her child is. But a mother can predict what her child will do now based on her childs's personality traits. If boy was interested to play games most probable boy must be near PlayStation. If the child do not like to read books, it's less probability to see him near reading section. All this the mother can

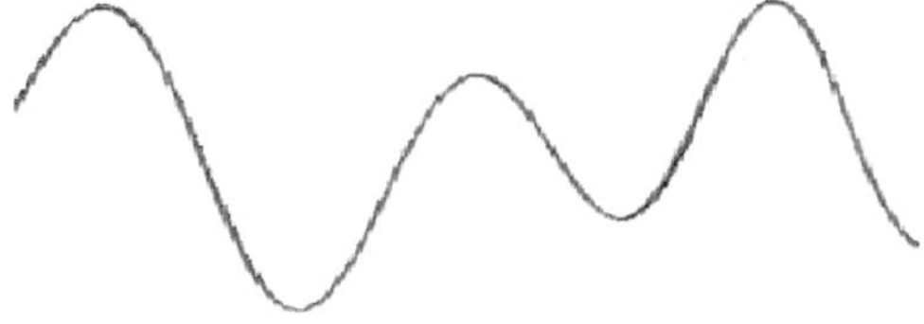

understand by the nature of the child. Like this the mother can predict every possibility where her child can be. The wave function for the child was shown in the graph. As the height of graph increases it's more likely to see the child there. Waves like these are called as wave functions.

Now imagine, if the mother suddenly opens the door. Mother would get the information where her child was sitting exactly, this time the wave function collapses. Mother has exact idea what and where his child is, so she don't need a probability wave hence the wave function collapses.

One thing to note here is, in this graph we can see negative amplitude. To get probability of a wave function we have to square the wave function thus we will get probability distribution wave.

A wave function defines each and every properties of quantum mechanics. An equation which controls all these wave functions is called Schrodinger wave equation. This equation was discovered by Ervin Schrodinger. Schrodinger maybe familiar to us with his Schrodinger's cat equation. But his major contribution to quantum mechanics was not his thought experiment called cat in a box. His major contribution was this wave equation.

Now let's get back to quantum mechanics. Let's assume if we trap an electron in a box. The specialty of this box is, the electron can only move in any one direction, only to left and right. The electron can't move in forward, backward, up and down when the electron was in box. Due to the wave nature of electron, it will not just sit in one place, it will keep moving in left and right inside the box. This movement will depend on the energy of the electron. This movement of electron can be represented in the form of waves. But the meaning of waves in quantum mechanics was different than classical mechanics. The probability to see the electron inside the box was not same everywhere. These waves in quantum mechanics represent the probability to see where an electron is.

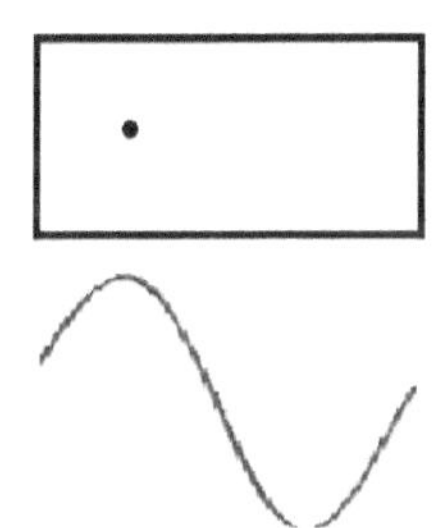

For an example. The wave represent the probability to show the movement of electron inside the box. If we square the wave, we will get a wave form like this, this newly obtained wave form is called probability distribution wave. It the height of the wave increases that means it's most probable to see the electron there. Which means we will get the information where the electron can be or cannot be. Here we discussed a wave function representing an electron which can only move and left and right. But in real life electron moves in 3 Dimensions. It can move in left, right, up, down, front and back, so a wave function representing this electron will be also a 3 dimensional wave.

The thing we have to understand here is when we say wave it doesn't mean the electron was travelling as a wave. It means the probability to see an electron through its movement. When we say waves in quantum mechanics it doesn't mean classical waves like water wave or sound waves. Quantum waves are probability waves. There is no need to be its position only, it can be any property. In quantum mechanics we represent every quantum property as these waves. Till now no one have understood how these waves works practically. Even though we haven't understood it, we can predict every property of quantum mechanics by these waves, and those prediction were proven by experimental results. That's why these waves and wave equations are still in use.

9. Quantum entanglement

In 1930 Albert Einstein provoked an opposition to a major discovery in quantum mechanics. He even called it as a spooky action. The idea of quantum entanglement was that, two physical bodies can transfer their information instantaneously meaning faster than speed of light. Einstein strongly opposed this idea. Because, Einstein's theories says nothing can travel faster than light. Then how quantum entanglement can transfer something faster than speed of light.

As usual let's understand entanglement with a real life example. Imagine we are shoe wearers, we know that the shoe on the right foot only fits on the right foot and the shoe on the left foot only fits on the left foot. Each foot have its own shoe. Then I bought a pair of shoes, and each shoe is packed in two different boxes. Imagine if one of the box is carried out to America by an American friend and other box is in India near you. Both boxes was not packed by you neither your American friend, so no one knows which shoe was in which box. You will have no idea which shoe is with me until you open your box right? As well American friend also will have no idea which shoe is with him until he opens it. When you opens your box you will get information about which shoe is with you. If you understood which shoe is with you, then you will get a clear idea of which shoe is with American friend, even without opening his box. This is a relationship, because shoes are a pair.

Let's look at another example. If you have two coins in your hand, specialty of these coins is that if you toss a coin and gets head, if so then when you toss other coin you will get tail. When one coin results head other will result tail. Each coins gives only opposite results. Practically this was not possible. When we toss a coin there is 50 percent chance to it be head or tail. We may get any result from any coin. But as we said first if we want to get opposite results. There must be a connection in between those coins. We will get opposite results only if there is a connection between those coins. Keep this in mind and read the rest.

When we say about quantum mechanics we study about sub atomic particles. Especially fundamental particles like electrons, photons.... Each of this particle has its own identity. We all have identities like height, weight, size… like this sub atomic particles too have their own identities depending upon its properties. Even two electron in an atom have its own different identities. Spin, angular momentum, magnetic momentum,

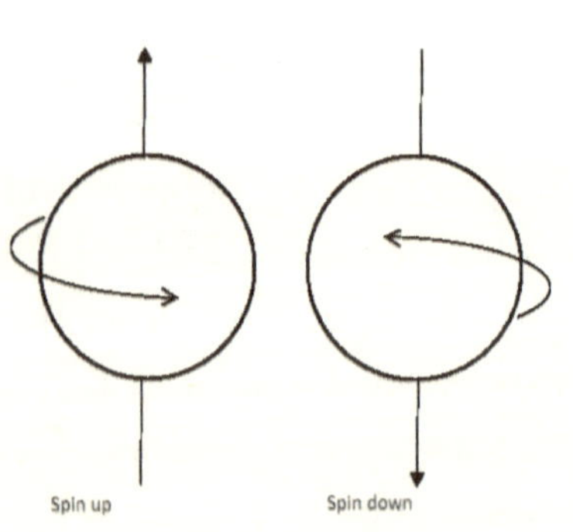

energy… are identities of sub atomic particles. Let's take spin for simplicity, spin means rotation of a body. Every spinning body had its own angular momentum, angular momentum was a property of a spinning body. Electron too shows angular momentum. So we assume electron has a spin, we don't know either if it was any other property of electron. Anyway assume electrons too have spin. We can measure this spin in two possible ways. Clockwise or anti clockwise or we could say it as up spin or down spin. If it was rotating in clockwise it is said to be down spin and if it was in anticlockwise direction it is said to be up spin.

Now let's take wave function, if we know a wave function of an electron we could understand its properties also. If two electrons have same wave function we can say both of them are entangled. Which means there exist some relationship between them. It two electron are said to be entangled they have some specialties.

If we split a sub atomic particle into two both of them would be entangled. Because their exist a wave function before the particle got split, that wave function will be same for both splitted particles. That means they are entangled. If we have such entangled pair, they will have a relationship in between them doesn't matter how long they are separated. They can transfer information faster than speed of light. We may get wondered when we hear something is travelling faster than the speed of light, we know nothing will travel faster than the speed of light, we had proved it with experimental proofs. Then how these information travels faster than speed of light?

If we took an entangled pair both of them will be in a superposition state until we try to observe any of it. If we observe one of its spin then we know that the other would spin in its opposite direction. Like this an entangled pair spin in all of its possible ways, it was in a superposition stage, but when we observe its spin, its wave function collapse and it will give a result, if we get a result we know that its entangled pair will have its opposite spin.

If we place an entangled particle in sun and another in earth, then by observing the particle which was placed in earth shows a result, at the same time or instantaneously we can understood the result of the entangled particle placed in sun. Remember even light from sun reaches earth only after eight minutes.

And so on Einstein and his two post doc fellows, Podolsk and Rosen these there came up with a theory to contradict quantum entanglement. They introduced a new variable called as hidden variable. They argued these entangled particles are pre-determined. The electron has already determined which spin to choose at the time when they get separated, they are not passing any information after their separation.

But with the emergence of Bell's inequality theory, they discovered that there is nothing exist as hidden variables. Which means there is nothing like hidden variable or nothing influences these entangled pairs at the time of separation, like Einstein said. It only depends the result of the particle we are observing, if the particle we are observing shows a result, its entangled pair will give its opposite result. It only depends on our observation. If we don't try to observe any of it both will stay in superposition state.

Now let's thing whether it travels faster than the speed of light. Before starting to think about the information let's think about does it transfer any information. That means it is random when we observe any of the entangled particle, the particle we observing can be up spin or down spin, it is a random choice, it can be in any spin. The spin of the observed particle was not chosen by us, it is just a random selection. We don't have any control over the observed particle, we can't say the particle must be in up or in down spin, we can't influence their spin. Because we don't know when we observe the particle how it collapses its wave function and how it chooses its spin. The result is random. We can't sent an information by influencing the entangled particle. But even though when we say they are random, there is some connection between them. We can't influence or manipulate that connection. But by using this random result we had already developed some technologies, quantum cryptography, quantum computer, quantum internet, quantum atomic clocks....

For the simplicity of understanding, here we had only talked about the spinning property of sub atomic particles. These particles have several another properties, which are a little bit complicated, those can also be explained same as spin.

10. Cat in a box

The essence of this thought experiment is to show the imperfections of quantum mechanics. Which means all the subatomic elementary particles are in a position called super position.

It is a thought experiment developed by Schrodinger to explain the quantum mechanical system. The experiment was conducted on a sealed box. Sealed box means, there is no way to get to know what's happing inside the box or the box will not transfer any information to the observer until the sealed box is opened.

So like as we said, we have a sealed box. Inside the sealed box there is an experimental setup like a bottle of poison is placed which can be break by a hammer and the hammer is connected in series to a Geiger counter which can detect radioactive decay and a radioactive decay material was also placed inside the box.

When the Radioactive material emits radiation which will be detected by the detector then the hammer is allowed to break the poison bottle. But the probability for the radioactive element to emit radiation is 50 percent and which is a random thing. No one can predict when will a radioactive element decays and emit radiation. That means for every half-life of time we have only 50 percent probability for the nucleus to decay.

So what Schrodinger ask is if we place a cat inside such a box with all experimental setup and leave the box for a while. How could we know whether the cat is alive or not. This is called Schrodinger cat paradox.

Scientists came up with a lot of explanations for this paradox. Among them the most accepted solution is Copenhagen interpretation. He explains sub atomic particles can exist in different place at once, and different sub atomic sates at one place also. Sub atomic particles have some properties like this. So why Schrodinger develop this thought experiment is because he was thinking about a quantum system which state is similar to the state of cat meaning quantum system's state cannot be predicted. Here if we take the sealed box as a quantum mechanical system then according to Copenhagen interpretation that cat exist as a superposition of dead and alive states like different subatomic states at one place. Concluding if you have a quantum mechanical system, then that system will exist as the superposition of all the existing particles inside the box. So the next question is does this superposition state exist forever. Whatever happens we need a result, because experimentally we can get into a result. So Copenhagen also concludes that whenever we try to observe the system that system itself will go to a single state of any of the superposition states. Whenever an observer measures a quantum mechanical system then that system will select any of the available superposition states and the whole system accept that state as its states. In here if we open the system (Box) the cat in superposition will attain any one state either dead or alive.

So according to Copenhagen interpretation a quantum mechanical system exist in superposition of its all possible states. And that superposition breakdown when we observe the system and reaches to any one of the states.

So in a simple way lets imagine you the reader was a quantum mechanical system, you can be a son, daughter, husband, wife, father or mother. So you can be all of this. Meaning you are in a superposition of all of these states. So if someone need to know who you are, then they need to approach you, for them you maybe father, mother, friend or anyone. So if your father came to you asking who you are? you will accept son states from the all above superposition states.

11. Quantum computing

In 1980s one of the most important physicists of 20th century forced to encounter a problem in physics. Richard Feynman was searching a door to enter to the quantum universe, because nature of quantum system in universe is to hide information from us. So if he want to observe quantum events he was forced to build a machine which was capable to simulate a quantum system. But soon he realized classical computers were not capable to build a system like this. Classical computers doesn't have the capability to solve the complexity of a quantum system that are hidden from us in nature.

Suddenly he got another idea. He thought to build a computer with quantum particles instead of classical mechanical particles. A computer which works according to the laws of quantum mechanics itself. Then it would be best suitable way to study about the mysteries of quantum mechanics, he thought.

A classical computers works on the basics of binary codes. That is 1, 0 or on, off stages. Classical computers can only exist in any one of this stages. Which means for an example, humans can laugh as well as cry, if we consider laugh is a state and cry is another state. Humans cannot exist in both state at a time, either in laugh or in cry state. And in the real quantum computer world a state is a position which we had discussed earlier. Like the same classical computer can only exist in any one of the stages cannot exist in both stages. Therefore classical computers can only perform only one calculation at a time. But we can't figure it out, we may feel like computers may loading several application at a time. It is because the time required to do a single calculation was very less in an average a classical computer can perform a calculation in under 1 nanosecond. Here the problem arises for the classical computers.

Quantum computers works on another principle. Language for quantum computers was not binary. Quantum computers use quantum bits also called as qubit. Qubit can exist in both 1, 0 or on, off states not only in any one of the state but both. If we look at the example we said above, that humans can laugh and cry at same time is called a qubit. This property was called as superposition which we discussed earlier. Why this is special is because it can perform more than one calculation at a time because it can accept both states.

If we give a way puzzle calculation to a classical computer it first tries its first solution and then the other solution, it repeats this step until it get a final solution, it performs single calculations at a time, next calculation was done only after completing the previous one. Let's assume if it takes 1 second to perform a calculation and it takes 10 calculations it will done its task in 10 seconds. But if this work was given to a quantum computer it can perform each and every possible calculations at a time. Which means it only take 1 second to perform the whole task.

60

THE END!

62